THE HISTORY OF THE
MARITIME WARS OF THE TURKS

PRINCETON SERIES OF MIDDLE EASTERN SOURCES IN TRANSLATION

General Editor, M. Şükrü Hanioğlu

THE HISTORY
OF THE
MARITIME WARS
OF THE TURKS

By
Kâtip Çelebi

Expanded, edited, and annotated by
Svatopluk Soucek

 Markus Wiener Publishers
Princeton

Originally printed for the Oriental Translation Fund, London, 1831
First reprinting, 1968, by the Johnson Reprint Corporation, New York

Cover image: The Battle of Preveza.

For information, write to:
Markus Wiener Publishers
231 Nassau Street, Princeton, NJ 08542
www.markuswiener.com

Library of Congress Cataloging-in-Publication Data

Kâtip Çelebi, 1609-1657.
   [Tuhfetü'l-kibâr fî esfâri'l-bihâr. English]
   The history of the maritime wars of the Turks / translated from the
Turkish of Kâtip Çelebi by James Mitchell ; expanded, edited, and
annotated by Svatopluk Soucek.
      p. cm.
   Includes bibliographical references.
   ISBN 978-1-55876-547-4 (hbk. : alk. paper)
   ISBN 978-1-55876-548-1 (pbk. : alk. paper)
   1. Turkey—History, Naval. 2. Turkey—History—1453-1683.
   I. Mitchell, James. II. Soucek, Svatopluk. III. Title.
   DR451.K3713 2011
   359.4'80956—dc23
                                    2011034141µ

Markus Wiener Publishers books are printed in the United States of America on acid-free paper and meet the guidelines for permanence and durability of the Committee on Production Guidelines for Book Longevity of the Council on Library Resources.

CONTENTS

v

LIST OF ILLUSTRATIONS

Illustrations from the Princeton University Library Manuscript Copy of
Tuhfet ül-Kibar fi Esfar il-Bihar **and from the 1329/1913 Printed Edition.**

Pages 11 – 27

First page of the Princeton University Library manuscript copy of *Tuhfet ül-Kibar fi Esfar il-Bihar.*
  Islamic Manuscripts New Series 1011. Manuscripts Division, Department of Rare Books and Special Collections, Princeton University Library.

World map from the Princeton University Library manuscript copy of *Tuhfet ül-Kibar fi Esfar il-Bihar.*
  Islamic Manuscripts New Series 1011. Manuscripts Division, Department of Rare Books and Special Collections, Princeton University Library.

Map of the Mediterranean Sea from the Princeton University Library manuscript copy of *Tuhfet ül-Kibar fi Esfar il-Bihar.*
  Islamic Manuscripts New Series 1011. Manuscripts Division, Department of Rare Books and Special Collections, Princeton University Library.

Map of the Adriatic and Aegean Seas from the Princeton University Library manuscript copy of *Tuhfet ül-Kibar fi Esfar il-Bihar.*
  Islamic Manuscripts New Series 1011. Manuscripts Division, Department of Rare Books and Special Collections, Princeton University Library.

An Ottoman World map.
  Kâtip Çelebi, *Tuhfet ül-Kibar fi Esfar il-Bihar* ([İstanbul]: Matbaa-yı Bahriye, 1329 [1913])

An Ottoman map of the Mediterranean with a compass rose.
  Kâtip Çelebi, *Tuhfet ül-Kibar fi Esfar il-Bihar* ([İstanbul]: Matbaa-yı Bahriye, 1329 [1913])

An Ottoman chart of the Aegean, with a compass rose.
  Kâtip Çelebi, *Tuhfet ül-Kibar fi Esfar il-Bihar* ([İstanbul]: Matbaa-yı Bahriye, 1329 [1913])

"The Gulf of Venice" (Venedik Körfezi), an Ottoman map of the Adriatic with a compass rose.
Kâtip Çelebi, *Tuhfet ül-Kibar fi Esfar il-Bihar* ([İstanbul]: Matbaa-yı Bahriye, 1329 [1913])

Compass roses.
Kâtip Çelebi, *Tuhfet ül-Kibar fi Esfar il-Bihar* ([İstanbul]: Matbaa-yı Bahriye, 1329 [1913])

A portrait of Venice based upon a map in the *Kitab-i Bahriye* of Piri Reis.
Kâtip Çelebi, *Tuhfet ül-Kibar fi Esfar il-Bihar* ([İstanbul]: Matbaa-yı Bahriye, 1329 [1913])

Barbarossa in the heat of battle.
Kâtip Çelebi, *Tuhfet ül-Kibar fi Esfar il-Bihar* ([İstanbul]: Matbaa-yı Bahriye, 1329 [1913])

Barbarossa's flag (*bayrak*), lantern (*fener*), and turban (*kavuk*).
Kâtip Çelebi, *Tuhfet ül-Kibar fi Esfar il-Bihar* ([İstanbul]: Matbaa-yı Bahriye, 1329 [1913])

Seydi Ali Reis's voyage from Basra to India.
Kâtip Çelebi, *Tuhfet ül-Kibar fi Esfar il-Bihar* ([İstanbul]: Matbaa-yı Bahriye, 1329 [1913])

"Sıngın Donanma Harbı" (The Battle of the Defeated Ottoman Fleet): Two representations of the Battle of Lepanto.
Kâtip Çelebi, *Tuhfet ül-Kibar fi Esfar il-Bihar* ([İstanbul]: Matbaa-yı Bahriye, 1329 [1913])

"Sıngın Donanma Cengi" (The Battle of Lepanto).
Kâtip Çelebi, *Tuhfet ül-Kibar fi Esfar il-Bihar* ([İstanbul]: Matbaa-yı Bahriye, 1329 [1913])

An Ottoman galley.
Kâtip Çelebi, *Tuhfet ül-Kibar fi Esfar il-Bihar* ([İstanbul]: Matbaa-yı Bahriye, 1329 [1913])

**Illustrations of Events, People, Places, and Ships
Mentioned in the Text of** *Tuhfet ül-Kibar fi Esfar il-Bihar.*

Pages 125 – 136

Kemal Reis in battle with Venetians (1499).
Süleyman Nutki, *Muharebat-ı Bahriye-i Osmaniye* (İstanbul: Bahriye Matbaası, 1307 [1890])

The Siege of Rhodes.
1522, Süleyman Nutki, *Muharebat-ı Bahriye-i Osmaniye* (İstanbul: Bahriye Matbaası, 1307 [1890])

Barbarossa Hayreddin.
Ali Rıza Seyfi, *Barbaros Hayreddin* ([İstanbul]: Bahriye Matbaası, 1330 [1914])

The Battle of Preveza: Barbarossa's and the Ottoman Empire's greatest naval victory.
Ali Rıza Seyfi, *Barbaros Hayreddin* ([İstanbul]: Bahriye Matbaası, 1330 [1914])

A galley under sail.
Ali Rıza Seyfi, *Turgut Reis* (İstanbul: İkbal Kütüphanesi, 1327 [1911])

A galley propelled by oars.
Ali Rıza Seyfi, *Turgut Reis* (İstanbul: İkbal Kütüphanesi, 1327 [1911])

Christian admiral's galley (*reale*).
Ali Rıza Seyfi, *Turgut Reis* (İstanbul: İkbal Kütüphanesi, 1327 [1911])

Andrea Doria, Barbarossa's and Turgut's archenemy.
Ali Rıza Seyfi, *Turgut Reis* (İstanbul: İkbal Kütüphanesi, 1327 [1911])

The fortress of Djerba.
Ali Rıza Seyfi, *Turgut Reis* (İstanbul: İkbal Kütüphanesi, 1327 [1911])

The Siege of Algiers by Charles V in 1541.
Ali Rıza Seyfi, *Turgut Reis* (İstanbul: İkbal Kütüphanesi, 1327 [1911])

Monks ransoming Christian captives in Algiers.
Ali Rıza Seyfi, *Turgut Reis* (İstanbul: İkbal Kütüphanesi, 1327 [1911])

PREFACE TO THE EXPANDED AND ANNOTATED EDITION

By Svatopluk Soucek

The *Tuhfet ül-Kibar fi Esfar il-Bihar* ("Gift to the Great Ones on the Subject of Maritime Campaigns") holds a special place in Ottoman Turkish historiography for two reasons. It is the story of the wars the Turks waged at sea during the entire span of the empire's expansion from the conquest of Constantinople to that of Crete (mid-fifteenth to mid-seventeenth century); and the subject has always fascinated scholars and the general reading public alike. If beyond the confines of Turkey Süleyman the Magnificent is probably the only readily recognized figure of Turkish history outside the orbit of professional historians, Hayreddin Barbarossa, the great corsair whom this sultan appointed commander of the imperial navy, most likely comes close to being another exception.

The author, Kâtip Çelebi (1609–1657), was a native of Istanbul whose real name was Mustafa bin Abdullah. Kâtip Çelebi could be translated as "Gentleman (Çelebi) Writer (Kâtip)"; it is a pen name by which he became commonly known on account of his prolific writing. In scholarly literature he also appears as Hacı Halife, because, on the one hand, he performed a pilgrimage (*hac*) to Mecca, becoming a *hacı*, pilgrim, and, on the other, he had an early career in the government's financial and accounting sector where the position he occupied had the title *halife*. He was the quintessential Ottoman intellectual, whose erudition spanned the entire range of traditional Muslim learning: theology, law, history, and literature. The Istanbul of his time was the populous capital of a great Islamic empire, where an educated man's curiosity could find a plethora of libraries with

1

books to read and a host of scholars whose lectures he could attend and with whom he could engage in stimulating debates. Kâtip Çelebi was only one of many similar personalities, but he stood out for his creative urge to organize and reformulate through his own writing what he had learnt. His scholarly output became prodigious, especially in the fields of history and bibliography. *Fezleke*, a history of the world, and *Kesf ez-Zünun*, a bibliography of Muslim books, are valuable sources still used today. All that made him remarkable, but not unique: other Muslim authors produced similarly abundant and valuable work. Where he rose above all others, however, was his interest in the world beyond the confines of Islam, and his desire to familiarize his coreligionists with it through works on geography and cartography. To find his peers among Muslims, we might have to reach back half a millennium before Kâtip Çelebi to that admirable scientist, Biruni, or three centuries back to that amazing traveler, Ibn Battuta. One result of Kâtip Çelebi's wide-ranging interests was *Cihannüma* ("Cosmography"); *Levami un-Nur*, the translation of a Dutch atlas, was another.[1] Had he lived longer, he no doubt would have continued and expanded this kind of scholarly output. He died, alas, at the relatively early age of forty-eight, probably of a stroke.

At the same time, Kâtip Çelebi remained a devout Muslim and a loyal citizen of the Ottoman Empire. His interest in the study of geography and cartography that was flourishing in the European West was motivated not only by intellectual curiosity but also by his conviction that in order to compete with contemporary Christian Europe, Ottoman Turks needed to possess a clear knowledge of the world around their empire. Six sultans occupied the throne during his lifetime: Ahmet I, Mustafa I, Osman II, Murat IV, Ibrahim, and Mehmet IV. In 1606, three years before he was born, Sultan Ahmet I and his Habsburg counterpart, Emperor Rudolph II, approved the peace treaty of Sitva Torok which put an end to a war that had dragged on since 1593. It marked the end of one era and the opening of a new one: instead of another Ottoman conquest, this war produced a stalemate, and the sultan saw himself obliged to recognize the Habsburg emperor as his equal in diplomatic negotiations. The age of expansion was inexorably drawing to a close, and the few flourishes yet to come quickly collapsed, only dramatizing this decline. Kâtip Çelebi witnessed one such flourish, and it was more a reconquest than a conquest: the energetic Murat IV's Baghdad campaign in 1638–1639, in which the Sunni sultan regained Iraq from his perennial Shi'a adversary, the shah of Iran.

There was one exception, however—the conquest of Crete. It was special for several reasons. Crete, a large island situated in a geostrategically crucial part of the eastern Mediterranean, was still in infidel hands, for Venice owned it as the last precious possession of her once extensive maritime empire. Had Murat IV lived longer, Crete might have been his next target after Iraq, and indeed there were moments when war with the republic almost broke out over incidents that were symptoms of the gathering storm. Murat died in 1640, however, and his brother, Ibrahim, who succeeded him on the throne, lacked the mettle that might have carried out this project with any degree of speed and efficiency. It became Kâtip Çelebi's lot to witness a drama the likes of which had never occurred before: an amphibious campaign that would last a whole generation, from 1645 to 1669. The author of the *Tuhfet ül-Kibar* did not live to see the successful conclusion of this campaign, for he died in 1657. The protracted and laborious nature of this war, which for a number of years repeatedly brought the adversary's fleets to the threshold of the Ottoman capital, the Dardanelles, both disturbed him and made him recall glorious exploits of Turkish mariners of the past. They were of two kinds: those of the seafaring *gazis*, corsairs waging *jihad* or holy war against infidel shipping and coasts, and those of official campaigns during which in the days of Süleyman the Magnificent the imperial fleet criss-crossed the whole expanse of the Mediterranean all the way to the coasts of France and Spain. Writing the story of this seaborne epic may have provided Kâtip Çelebi with particular consolation in the face of the Ottoman navy's current travails. Having done that, the author could not resist adding a long section on various aspects of naval matters, again partly historical (a list of the *kaptanpaşas*, admirals at the command of the imperial fleet); partly topical (the types of ships used in the fleet, the kinds of navigational tools and shipbuilding materials, the rules—*kanun*—regulating the annual sailings of the imperial fleet); and partly didactic (advice on how to proceed in a variety of situations, such as when confronting enemy ships and fleets). As a young civil servant,

Kâtip Çelebi had participated in grueling wars on the Iranian frontier, but he never took part, as far as is known, in any venture at sea; the fact that he was able to write this remarkable book is additional testimony to the wonder that was Istanbul during his time—depository of a wealth of government records to which he had access, home to the imperial arsenal where he may have had acquaintances, the many mariners he could meet in the Ottoman capital.

For the main, historical section of the *Tuhfet ül-Kibar*, however, Kâtip Çelebi's sources were accounts like *Tac ut-tevarih*, a chronicle compiled by Hoca Sadeddin, a high-level official who wrote at the end of the sixteenth century, and narratives based on personal experience and reminiscences written by the mariners themselves (or ghost-written for them). The latter category was dominated by the autobiography of the greatest of them all, the *Gazavat* ("Holy War Campaigns") of Hayreddin Barbarossa. It is a captivating story and an important document on several levels. One is personal: the life of a Turkish sailor who from modest beginnings as a seafaring merchant in his home waters of the Aegean Sea had risen by 1520 to become the founder of the great corsair regency of Algiers, loyal to the Ottoman sultan and a scourge of the Infidels over the entire expanse of the maritime combat zone—the central and western Mediterranean. Another is its account of the campaigns of the imperial fleet, after Sultan Süleyman had appointed him chief admiral in 1534. The *Gazavat* was thus the basis for the most dramatic segment of the *Tuhfet ül-Kibar*.

Another source at Kâtip Çelebi's disposal was the famous *Kitab-i Bahriye* or "Book on Maritime Matters," written by Barbarossa's contemporary, Piri Reis. No less valuable than the *Gazavat* as a historical document, the *Kitab-i Bahriye* also radically differs from it, for it is a book of sailing directions and descriptions of coasts and islands throughout the entire Mediterranean. The *Kitab-i Bahriye* is unique in its comprehensiveness and stated purpose, for the author's goal was to provide his Turkish seafaring coreligionists with useful, often indispensable knowledge.

These and other sources used by Kâtip Çelebi limit themselves to the Mediterranean; a few, however, also encompass the Indian Ocean, where the Ottoman Turks ventured less often; in fact, they had turned their backs on it by the time he wrote this book. The author tells the story of Ottoman maritime wars there as well, and one of his principal sources was the *Mir'at ül-Memâlik* or "Mirror of Countries," Seydi Ali Reis's account of his attempt to bring an Ottoman fleet from the Persian Gulf to Suez but which the Portuguese and storms deflected to India.

The popularity of the *Tuhfet ül-Kibar* among Kâtip Çelebi's countrymen is attested by the number of known extant manuscript copies: thirty-one, besides two incomplete ones. Most, if not all, must have been copied between 1657 and 1729. The latter date is that of the first printed edition published in Istanbul by Ibrahim Müteferrika, founder of the Daru't-Tıbâ'ati'l-Ma'mûre, the earliest Muslim printing venture. A second edition was published in Istanbul by Matbaa-yı Bahriye in 1913. These two are the only printed versions of the original Ottoman Turkish text in Arabic script. A modernized version in Roman alphabet (*yeni yazı*, the script of modern Turkish) was made by Orhan Şaik Gökyay, who also supplemented it with a valuable introduction, annotation, and other ancillary materials (Istanbul: Tercüman, 1980). Oddly, until a few years ago, there was no complete translation into any language of this important source and engaging chronicle. In English, only a partial translation exists: *The History of the Maritime Wars of the Turks, Translated from the Turkish of Haji Khalifeh by James Mitchell. Chapters I to IV.* London: Printed for the Oriental Translation Fund, 1831. It covers the first two thirds of the book.

* * * * *

Our project took root with the decision by Markus Wiener, as advised by William Blair, that—given the interest in the book and the fact that James Mitchell's translation, however truncated, has continued to serve as a frequently cited source—a reprint would be worthwhile, provided that adequate ancillary material was included: a new preface, a summary of the chapters constituting the missing third, and a commentary or annotation. I was asked to join the project as the person who would prepare these additions. It was at this point that we discovered the existence of a new English translation published in Ankara: Kâtib Çelebi, *The Gift to the Great Ones on Naval Campaigns*, edited by Prof. Idris Bostan, Ankara: Prime Ministry Undersecretary for Maritime Affairs, 2008. This translation, completed by Uzman Tercüme Ltd. Şirketi, is part of a sumptuous presentation that includes, on the one hand, a long and many-faceted scholarly apparatus (an introduction, a thorough account of Kâtip Çelebi's life, a description of all his works, a still more detailed discussion of the *Tuhfet* itself, a list and description of all known manuscripts, annotations, bibliographies, and indexes, and a number of reproductions of maps found in several manuscripts) and, on the other hand, a facsimile reproduction of TSMK Revan 1192, the 1657 manuscript considered the earliest, from which the English translation was made. Moreover, a CD-ROM disk accompanies this publication. At the same time, a parallel edition with, instead of an English translation, a transcription of the Turkish text in *yeni yazı* (thus, not a modernization of the language itself, which would have duplicated Gökyay's modernized version) has been issued.

That should have spelled the end of our project, but once we were able to actually examine the new English translation from Ankara, we realized that it in no way negated the desirability of publishing the version we had in mind. The size and cost (about $400) of the bulky Ankara edition diminishes its accessibility and usefulness to the wider public; clearly, the publishers as well as the editors had two select

PREFACE TO THE EXPANDED EDITION

kinds of clientele in mind: the institutional one—great public and academic libraries, museums, government offices—and the sophisticated layperson alert to the heritage of Ottoman civilization who at the same time has the means to acquire this expensive book, which also fulfills the function of a "coffee-table" edition. Furthermore, the disadvantage of limited accessibility is compounded by other, quite unexpected problems. In one sense the presentation is scholarly, but the extensive ancillary segment includes an excessive number of rather irrelevant details, while failing to provide enough of the kind of information that most readers would have found useful for a proper understanding of the text.[2]

Beyond the aforementioned weaknesses, one more stands out: no effort was made to adapt the English version to the needs of its readers—virtually all the references are to an often arcane bibliographic apparatus exclusively in Turkish or Arabic and located in Turkey, while ignoring the rich secondary literature in Western languages, to say nothing of often abundant primary sources. This lack of attentiveness may also explain the at-first-sight somewhat intriguing statement on page 50: "Since the language of the work is the Turkish of the period and quite understandable, we have not simplified it according to modern Turkish and the expressions of Kâtib Çelebi have been preserved." This sentence makes no sense in the English translation, but it does acquire meaning when we realize that it is a mechanical translation of the introduction to the parallel Turkish version of this publication.

General Description of Kâtip Çelebi's *Tuhfet ül-Kibar*

The *Tuhfet ül-Kibar* consists of two parts (*kısım*): the first part is narrative, the history proper; the second part is topical, covering various aspects of naval matters. Each of the two parts is divided into chapters (*fasıl*); there are nine chapters in the first part, seven chapters in the second. Only chapters 1 through 4 of the first part are present in Mitchell's translation.

What Is Included in This Edition

An accurate, well-annotated translation would be ideal, but the time such a project would require is beyond the range of our possibilities. A more modest presentation is still worthwhile, we think, and the following elements are included in this edition:

a) A reprint of the 1831 translation, which encompasses the first two thirds of the text.
b) A summary of the chapters that constitute the missing third.
c) A translation of several excerpts from the missing third.
d) Commentary and notes on both the part covered by the 1831 translation, the summary of the final third, and the translated excerpts.
e) Maps and illustrations.
f) Bibliography.

Spelling and Transliteration

For Turkish names and words, we have adopted the latest system officially approved in Turkey (thus Kâtip and not Kâtib; Mehmet and not Mehmed). However, this system, even though demanded by law, is not always fully followed by the Turks themselves. Kâtip Çelebi's name in the edition published under the sponsorship of the Turkish government appears as Kâtib Çelebi. When we cite such publications, we of course have no choice but to do so faithfully.

The alphabet is the same as in English, except for the following differences: English j = Turkish c; English ch = Turkish ç; English sh = Turkish ş. Turkish ö is equivalent to French eu; Turkish ü is the same as its German sibling. Turkish undotted ı, a back vowel, is equivalent to Russian y. Turkish ğ is not pronounced but lengthens the preceding vowel.

Place names are presented generally in their most recognizable forms and those most likely to be found on standard maps. However, since it is often desirable to know other forms of certain names as well, we include them either in parentheses or in a footnote: thus, for example, Lesbos (Midilli); Little Malta (accompanied by a footnote: Küçük Malta in Turkish, Gozzo in Italian); and Navarino (accompanied by a footnote: Anavarin in Turkish, Pylos in Greek).

Illustrations from the
Princeton University Library
Manuscript Copy of
Tuhfet ül-Kibar fi Esfar il-Bihar
and from the 1329/1913
Printed Edition

First page of the Princeton University Library manuscript copy of
Tuhfet ül-Kibar fi Esfar il-Bihar.

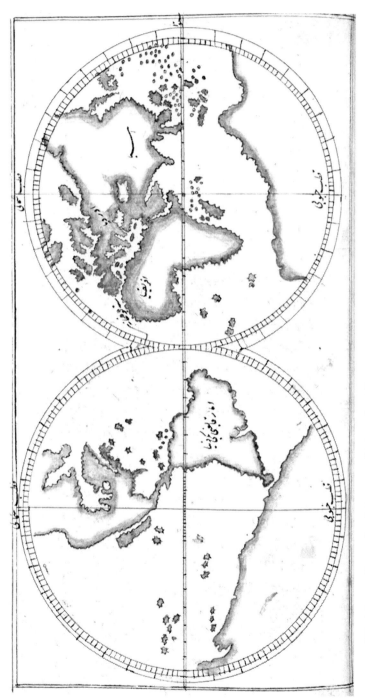

World map from the Princeton University Library manuscript copy of *Tuhfet ül-Kibar fi Esfar ül-Bihar.*

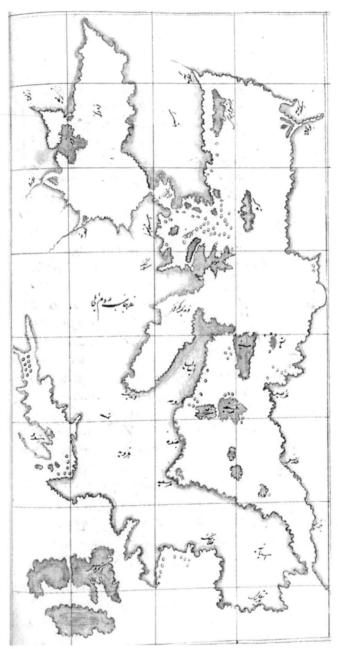

Map of the Mediterranean Sea from the Princeton University Library manuscript copy of *Tuhfet ül-Kibar fi Esfar il-Bihar.*

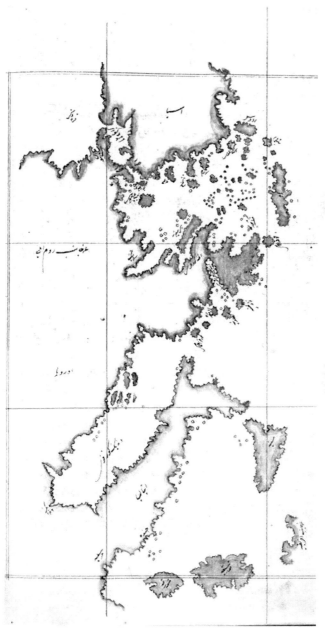

Map of the Adriatic and Aegean Seas from the Princeton University Library manuscript copy of *Tuḥfet ül-Kibar fi Esfar il-Bihar.*

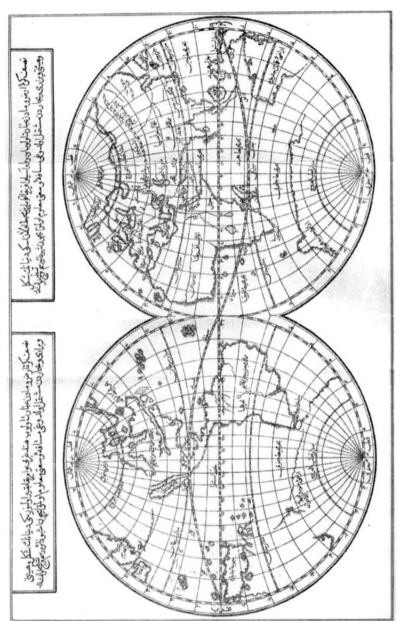

An Ottoman World map.

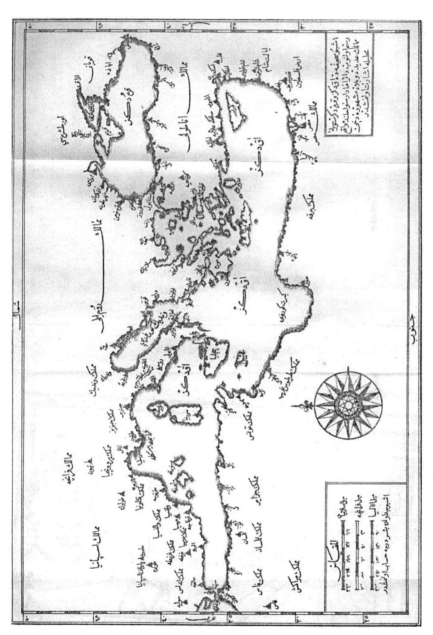

An Ottoman map of the Mediterranean with a compass rose.

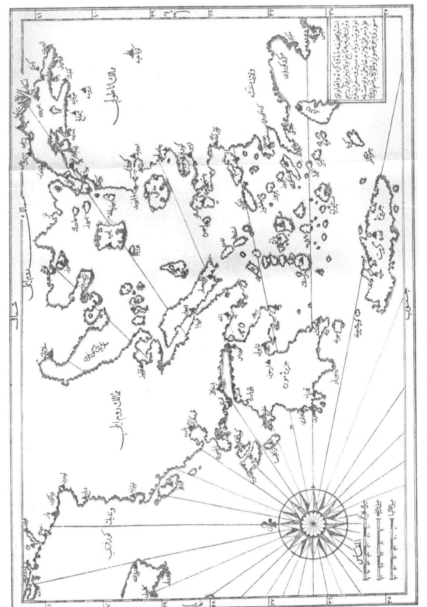

An Ottoman chart of the Aegean, with a compass rose.

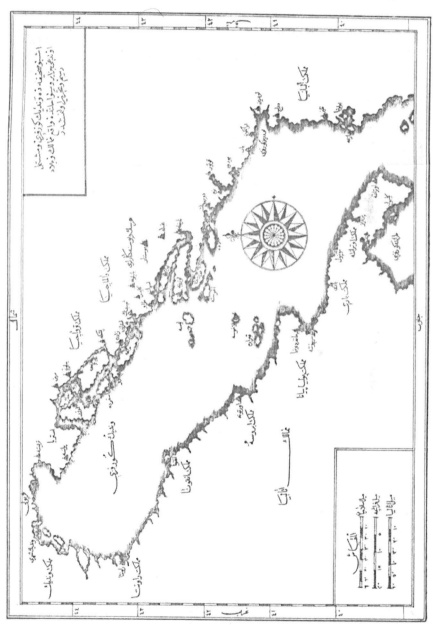

"The Gulf of Venice" (Venedik Körfezi), an Ottoman map of the Adriatic with a compass rose.

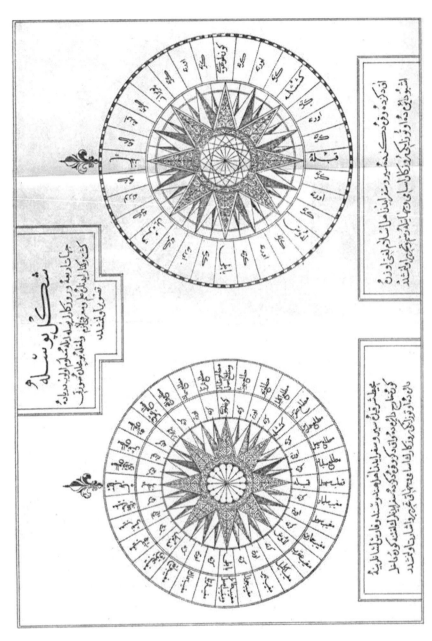

Compass roses.

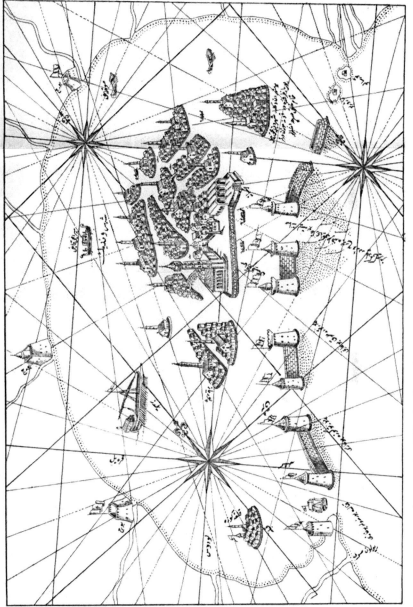

A portrait of Venice based upon a map in the *Kitab-i Bahriye* of Piri Reis.

Barbarossa in the heat of battle.

Barbarossa's flag (*bayrak*), lantern (*fener*), and turban (*kavuk*).

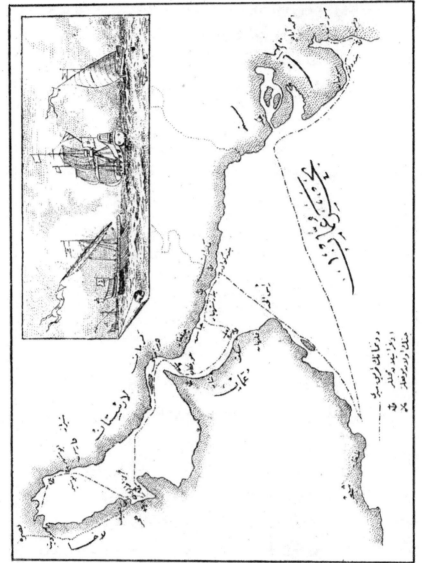

Seydi Ali Reis's voyage from Basra to India.

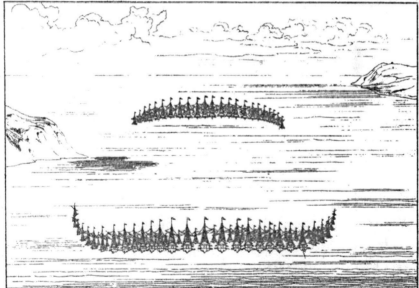

"Sıngın Donanma Harbı" (The Battle of the Defeated Ottoman Fleet):
Two representations of the Battle of Lepanto.

"Sıngın Donanma Cengi" (The Battle of Lepanto).

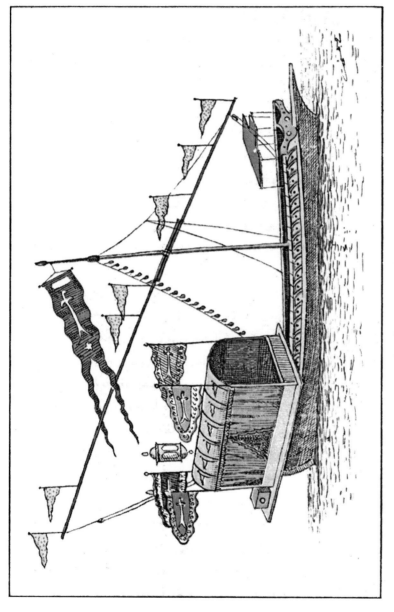

An Ottoman galley.

THE HISTORY OF THE MARITIME WARS OF THE TURKS

PART ONE

CHAPTERS I TO IV

THE

HISTORY

OF THE

MARITIME WARS OF THE TURKS,

TRANSLATED FROM

THE TURKISH OF HAJI KHALIFEH

BY JAMES MITCHELL.

CHAPTERS I. TO IV.

LONDON:

PRINTED FOR THE ORIENTAL TRANSLATION FUND,

BY A. J. VALPY, RED LION COURT, FLEET STREET.

SOLD BY J. MURRAY, ALBEMARLE STREET; AND MESSRS. PARBURY, ALLEN, AND CO.,
LEADENHALL STREET; MESSRS. THACKER AND CO., CALCUTTA; MESSRS. TREUTTEL
AND WÜRTZ, PARIS; AND MR. ERNEST FLEISCHER, LEIPSIG.

1831.

JOHNSON REPRINT CORPORATION   JOHNSON REPRINT COMPANY LTD.
111 Fifth Avenue, New York, N.Y. 10003   Berkeley Square House, London, W. 1

First reprinting, 1968, Johnson Reprint Corporation
Printed in the United States of America

TO

THE RIGHT HONORABLE

GEORGE JOHN EARL SPENCER, K.G. F.R.S. M.R.A.S.

&c. &c. &c.

THIS TRANSLATION

OF THE

HISTORY OF THE MARITIME WARS OF THE TURKS

IS, WITH HIS LORDSHIP'S PERMISSION,

MOST RESPECTFULLY INSCRIBED,

BY

HIS LORDSHIP'S GRATEFUL AND OBEDIENT SERVANT,

THE TRANSLATOR.

TRANSLATOR'S PREFACE.

THE work of which the following pages contain a translation was some time since recommended to the notice of the Oriental Translation Committee, by the venerable nobleman to whom this performance is inscribed, as being calculated to throw considerable light on the naval history of the Turkish nation.

It is entitled تحفة الكبار في اسفار البحار *A gift to the Great concerning Naval Expeditions.* The author, Haji Khalifeh,* is known to all Oriental scholars as a deliberate and impartial historian, and a man of extensive learning. In the present work, however, he has confined himself to a simple narration of events as they occurred, leaving to his readers the task of philosophising on their influence on the political affairs of the empire in general. Of his youthful days nothing is known, except that he was the son of a Sipahi, and that at an early age he was taught to read and write. In his twenty-fifth year he entered as student into the office of the chief historiographer; and while in this capacity,

---

* His entire name is مصطفي بن عبدالله حاجي خليفه Mustaffa Ben Abdullah Haji Khalifeh. He was also called كاتب چلبي Katib Chelebi.

was present in the Persian campaigns of Hamadan and Baghdad. On his return to Constantinople, he attended the lectures of Kazi-Zadeh. Whilst the army was wintering at Aleppo he made the pilgrimage to Mecca and Medina, whence his title of Haji, or Pilgrim. He was also at the siege of Erivan. He now commenced "the greater holy warfare," —that against ignorance, by indefatigable study. He attended the principal professors of the capital, and after ten years' application to the study of languages, the law, logic, and rhetoric, and the interpretation of the Koran and the traditions, he applied himself to the mathematics and geography, to which latter science the Cretan war particularly attracted his attention. At length, beginning to suffer from ill health, he devoted himself to the study of medicine and the mysteries of religion. So ardent was he in the pursuit of knowledge, that he frequently sat up whole nights reading some favourite author; and when he first commenced his literary labours, he expended the whole of his little patrimony in the purchase of books; but some time afterwards a rich relation died, leaving him a legacy, which enabled him to enjoy more of the comforts of life, and to make some additions to his library.

The fruits of his thirty years' study are the following excellent works: —a translation of the "Minor Atlas," under the title of "Rays of Light," which he translated from the Latin by the assistance of Shaikh Mohammed, a renegade Frenchman; "The View of the World," which contains the geography of Asia; and a "Description of European Turkey." These are the three best geographical productions of the Ottomans. They were succeeded by five historical works: two bearing the title "Fezliké;" the one in Arabic being an universal history from the creation of the world, till within three years of his death; the other, a similar history, in Turkish, from the year 1000 of the Hejirah (about which time he must have been born), also continued till three years before his death, being a period of sixty-five years; the "History of the

Maritime Wars;" a "History of Constantinople;" and the well-known "Chronological Tables." Then, his great Bibliographical and Encyclopædical Dictionary, which forms the groundwork of D'Herbelot's "Bibliotheque Orientale." Besides these, he wrote several smaller treatises, one of which, his last work, he entitled "True Scales for the Detection of Truth." This contains some curious essays on smoking, dancing, singing, &c., and concludes with a short account of himself.[*] He died at Constantinople in the month of Zilhijeh, A. H. 1068. (A. D. 1657.)

This work was the second which issued from the imperial printing-office, established at Constantinople in the year 1726, under the superintendence of Syed Effendi and Ibrahim Effendi; the latter a Hungarian, who had embraced the Mohammedan faith, and on whom the more immediate direction of the establishment seems to have devolved. The types, which were cast by him at Constantinople, are very neat, and the execution of the whole, considering that printing in Turkey was then only in its infancy, is highly creditable to the ingenuity of Ibrahim. Unfortunately, however, it abounds in typographical errors, which have frequently occasioned the translator considerable difficulty. In addition to a list of upwards of two hundred errata appended to the work, he has detected as many more, which were not corrected in a second impression which was subsequently printed.

The volume is a small folio, consisting of 149 pages, exclusive of the table of contents, the list of errata, and the printer's dedication, and is accompanied by five neatly executed plates, the first of which represents the two terrestrial hemispheres; the second, the Mediterranean and Black Seas; the third, the islands subject to the Ottoman empire; the fourth, the Adriatic; and the fifth, two mariner's compasses, one having

---

[*] To this work, and more especially to the invaluable "History of the Ottoman Empire," by J. Von Hammer, the translator is principally indebted for this biographical notice of the author.

the names of the winds in Turkish, the other both in Turkish and Arabic.

The translator has endeavoured to render his version as literal as possible. In some few instances, however, owing either to the errors of the press, or to the use of obsolete nautical terms, of which the most diligent inquiries made during a residence of some months in the capital of Turkey, failed to obtain him the explication, he may not have hit upon the precise signification: but these are few in number, and of such a nature as not to affect the general sense of the narrative.

He takes this opportunity of acknowledging his obligations to Omer Effendi, an officer of the pasha of Egypt, now in London, for the valuable assistance he has rendered him during the progress of the work.

London,
August 12th, 1831.

CONTENTS.

CHAPTER I.

b

x   CONTENTS.

CHAPTER II.

CONTENTS.

CHAPTER III.

CONTENTS.   xiii

HISTORY

OF

THE MARITIME WARS OF THE TURKS.

AUTHOR'S PREFACE.

In the Name of the Compassionate and Merciful God,—and on him we rely.

In commencing the History of the Conqueror of the World, it is proper that all due praise should be ascribed to the Lord of the Earth and Time, who, according to the signification of the sacred verse, "*Certainly my Hosts shall be victorious,*" hath strengthened the armies of the Faithful : and having by his revealed decree and promise, "*I will fill with awe the hearts of the Unbelievers,*" terrified the enemies of the Faith : has also by his command, "*When ye meet them be steady,*" rendered permanent the power and victory of the True Believers.

And salutations of joy and songs of peace be ascribed to our Prophet, the Lord of Creation, Mohammed Mustaffa, (upon whom be the peace of God!) who, by the divine Oracle, "*The cities shall be opened to you,*" preached his glorious religion, which he has bequeathed as an invaluable treasure to his illustrious household and posterity till the day of the resurrection. Thus, in confirmation of his divine prediction, in the year one thousand and fifty-five from the flight of the Prophet (A.D. 1645), amongst other victories, he vanquished the island of Candia; so that in the space of ten years its capital and all the other forts and towns came, one by one, into the hands of the Faithful. By these means several circumstances having transpired, which on some occasions, through negligence and want of management, tended to the advantage of the Infidels, the author of these pages, Haji Khalifeh, according to the verse of Muttanabbi, the prince of poets, "Thou hast no squadrons to bring forward, nor property to present; if therefore thy state is not happy, let at least thy words be acceptable," in order to manifest a zeal for religion, and the defence of the Faithful; and having in view the establishment of the Ottoman power, and the destruction of the Unbelievers, has related how the ancient kings spoke with maledictions on this subject, and the reasons of their rage and hatred; the battles of celebrated admirals and captains; the opinions and deliberations of the experienced and wise; and several other matters pertaining to expeditions and fleets. These he called, "A Gift to the Great respecting Naval Expeditions;" and having completed it, he presented it at the feet of the Lord of Munificence, the Illustrious of the World, the Sovereign of the Land and Ocean, Attendant of the two Holy Cities (Mecca and Medina), Sultan Mohammed Khan, son of Sultan Ibrahim Khan, (may God perpetuate his kingdom, and continue his power to the end of time!) with the hope that, considering its usefulness, he would be pleased to bestow his approbation.

This Epitome then consists of an Introduction, two parts, and a Conclusion.

INTRODUCTION.

RESPECTING the difficulties we have had in this work, the fixing of the boundaries, and drawing the maps of places:

Be it known, that to those engaged in the affairs of state, no science is so necessary as that of geography. If they are not acquainted with the whole surface of the earth, they ought at least to know the figure of the Turkish empire and the neighbouring states; that, when it may be necessary to undertake a journey, or to send an army into any country, they may be properly directed; and by this knowledge it will be easy to enter the enemy's territory, and defend their own frontiers. Persons ignorant of this science are not competent to be counsellors, even should they be natives; for there are many natives who are ignorant even of the figure of their own country and its boundaries.

Of the necessity of this science the following will be a sufficient proof; that the Infidels by application to it have discovered America, and become masters of India: and even the despicable Venetians, a nation the chief of which among the Christian kings is confined to the title of Duke, and is known by the epithet of *the Fisherman*, coming to the frontiers of the Ottoman empire, have opposed their power to that of our august Monarch, who rules from east to west.

In order therefore to illustrate this history of voyages, we shall in the first place give a map of the whole figure of the globe; then of the Mediterranean and Black Seas; and then of the countries of Venice and Germany. Thus, at first sight, a person may obtain a summary knowledge of the figure of the globe and the Turkish dominions; and being able to tell where the city of Venice, the castle of Zadra (Zara), or the island of Corfu, is situated, he will find it useful in commencing the perusal of travels and voyages. All the land and water of the globe are, according to the map, contained in two circles. The first circle represents half of the globe, and the ancient four quarters ; and the other circle is the other half, or more recently-discovered part which they call the new world.

EXPLANATION OF THE GLOBE.

The different portions of land on the surface of the globe, which by attraction or repulsion are found projecting through the element of water, are, according to the rules of geography, marked by red and yellow. The yellow represents the continent, the little red spots are islands, and the white shows the water. The line drawn across the two circles is the equator, and the double red line on each side of it is the ecliptic, showing the sun's extreme ascension and declension. Besides these are the zones, and the lines of latitude and longitude, by which the latitude and longitude of towns and the situation of places are ascertained. These I have explained at full length in my work called the *Jehan Nemah*,* which is the translation of an atlas. Here it will be sufficient to know, that every line is divided into three hundred and sixty degrees, and each degree into three stages (munzil), so that the whole circumference of the globe is 1080 stages ; and a person going west and moving forward will return by the east. This assertion has been corroborated by proof. To proceed : geographers divide the whole earth into four regions. They draw an imaginary line from the Mediterranean, the Strait of Constantinople, the Strait of Jenicale, and the south of the river Don as far as the Northern Ocean, and the region that remains on the west of this line they call Europe ; that on the east, Asia ; and the districts of Ethiopia and Egypt, which divide the Mediterranean and Red Seas, they call Africa. The new world they call America. The Ottoman power, then, has a share in each of the three regions. To exhibit these portions and their boundaries, I have drawn a map of the European portion and the Mediterranean and Black Seas, and described their boundaries. I have also marked the names of the Christian towns, and the Bosnia shores. When necessary it will be sufficient to show their situations.

EXPLANATION OF THE MAP.

The Mediterranean which is drawn on this map is, excepting the ocean, the largest of the six seas in the four quarters. It extends over ten degrees of latitude and thirty of longitude. From the Straits of Gibraltar in the east to the

---

* A compendious work on Geography, published at Constantinople, A. D. 1732.

Syrian coast, it is computed to be seventy degrees. On its southern coast are,
Fez, Tilimsan, Algiers, Tunis, Mahdiah, Jarba, Tripoli West, Alexandria of
Egypt, and Damietta. Its western and Arabian coast terminates at Arish. On
the east are, Gaza, Acca, Bairut, Tripoli Sham, and Pias. On the north, Selfeka,
Anemur, Alanieh, Antakia, and proceeding by Cape Teker and Smyrna as far as
the Strait (of the Dardanelles) are the coasts of Anatolia. It terminates at the
island of Boosja. From within the Strait as far as the Strait of Constantinople
is a small sea (Marmora) of about seven hundred miles in circumference. On
the coasts of this sea are, Kaputagh, Mikhalij, Moudania, Bay of Gemlik, Constantinople, Chekmejeh, and Gallipoli. Within it are the islands of Marmara,
Amar-Ali, and Kuzil. Beyond the Straits on the Rumelian shores are, the plain
of Aja, Enos, Cavalla, Aianur, Zlonkur, Kesendreh, Gulf of Salonica, the Gulfs
of Koolur and Azdin, the Negropont ; and in the Morea, Capes Napoli and
Menkesheh (or St. Angelo), which, as Cape Teker in Anatolia, form an
angle and passage (with Candia). Projecting from the land into the sea, they
extend nearly to the east and west points of Candia, and most of the islands of
the Mediterranean being within this centre, they call it (Candia) the central
island. All these islands have been taken from the Venetians and Genoese,
except Istandil (Tino) in the middle, which remains in the hands of the Venetians. That also was formerly captured, but for the sake of policy it was given
in exchange for the castle of Menkesheh (St. Angelo).

The names and situations of these islands are marked ; but to avoid prolixity,
I do not enter into a minute account of them, for my purpose is to explain the
Bosnia and Arnaout (Albanian) coasts. Leaving Cape Menkesheh and going
round the Morea, we pass Capes Manieh (Matapan), Modon, and Helomej.
The coast terminates at Badra (Patras). The whole of it is computed to be two
hundred miles.

THE VENETIAN ISLANDS ON THE COAST OF THE MOREA.

The principal islands near this coast, subject to the Venetians, are these :
Choka (Cerigo), fifteen miles south of Cape Menkesheh, and sixty miles in
circumference ; it has a strong castle. Zaklisa (Zante), fifteen miles west of
Helomej, is a rocky island, and has a strong fortress.

THE TOWNS ON THE ARNAOUT SHORES.

In the Atlas this country is called Albania. Fifty-six miles from the mouth of the Gulf of Lepanto is Prevesa; eighty miles from thence is the posterior part of Delvino; sixty beyond that Avlona; a hundred farther Duraj (Durazzo); and a hundred miles beyond that is Nuovo. On these shores, turning round from Port Injeer, in the island of Aiamur (Lefcathia) to the mouth of the Gulf of Narda (Arta), we first meet the castle of Prevesa. Next Parga, which is a castle belonging to the Venetians, situated on an elevated spot near the sea. Behind it is Mount Mizarak: to the east the country is rocky, and is interspersed with villages and water-mills. * Then, the port of Chinak, opposite the island of Corfu, is a celebrated harbour. It has lately been strengthened by having a fortress built in it. Next, passing a small arm of the sea, is Lake Dalianli, at the mouth of which is a castle belonging to the Venetians, rendered famous from its having been lately captured by one of the princes of that nation. To the north of Cape Durazzo are the castles of Lemesh, Eskanderieh, Oulkoun, Bar, Boudou, and Nuovo. The latter, which is situated in the Bay of Coutour (Cattaro), is called Castel Nuovo, which signifies a new castle. Eighteen miles farther, at the extreme end of the bay, is the castle of Cattaro, situated in the Ottoman dominions, but subject to Venice. It is built at the foot of a mountain, and a river passes it on both sides. Being a very strong castle, its capture has hitherto been found impracticable. The islands near these are, the two islands of Kefalonia (Cephalonia), situated opposite the mouth of the Gulf of Lepanto. Great Cephalonia is one hundred and fifty miles in circumference, and is a well-populated island. Its castle was once captured, but after the taking of Modon the Venetians again took possession of it. It is twenty miles east from Zante. Little Cephalonia (Theaki) is a small island to the north: it has no castle. Port Injeer in Aiamura (Lefcathia), is about six miles from Cephalonia. Then, opposite Parga is Bahshilar (Paxu), a pleasant little island of about thirty miles in circumference, and eighteen from the shore. We next come to the island of Corfu, which extends from Delvino along the Mizarak shores. It is about forty miles from Parga, and its castle is six miles from Port Chinak. It is one hundred and ninety miles in circumference, is a celebrated and well-populated island, and has a strong fortress built in the sea, but connected on one side with the land. In former times this island passed by right of inheritance from one of the Christian princes who governed Albania into the hands of a woman, but in A. H. 803 (A. D. 1400), the Venetians becoming victorious, succeeded by stratagem in wresting it from her, and having fortified the castle, they made it a guard island for the Gulf, and a general rendezvous for their army and navy. Near to it, in the mouth of the Gulf, is a watch-tower, and Kemal Reis

* *Aker sü dekermenler:* mills moved by running water.

observing that the Venetians had their eye upon it, repeatedly suggested to the late Sultan Soleiman Khan the necessity of capturing it; in consequence of which, in 943 of the Hejra (A. D. 1536), the illustrious emperor proceeded thither by sea and land, and completely besieged it. What followed shall be related in its proper place. The castle of Corfu, as described in the Bahria, is nearly three miles in circumference, is a very strong fort, and has within it and in the suburbs about eighteen thousand houses. Within the walls the Venetians have built, upon two hills, two towers of stone, with a subterraneous passage between them, so that when necessary they are able to render assistance to each other. Its walls are surrounded by the sea, and it has also a harbour, into which the smaller vessels enter, but the galleys lie outside. Between this island and the coast there is a small strait, by which when necessary an army may pass. The above-mentioned islands are the principal ones belonging to the Venetians, but there are besides them numerous little islands in the Gulf. Sixty miles below Corfu is Avlona, which is opposite Kara Beroun (in Anatolia) and Cape St. Maria (C. di Leuca) on the Polia shores, and from this place the sea is called the Gulf of Venice. It extends as far as the city of Venice in the north, is seven hundred miles in length, and about one hundred and fifty in breadth. On its eastern coast are the districts of Arnaout, Hersek (Herzegovinia), Bosnia, and Croatia. On the west, Lombardia, Ancona, and Poliapiana.

THE HERSEK AND BOSNIA SHORES.

Having passed Castel Nuovo, situated as before described on the Bay of Cattaro, and proceeding eighteen miles to the north, we come to the castle of Dobra-Venedik (Ragusa), situated in a district the inhabitants of which are an independent people, and whose territory extends from Hersek to Ghabla and Mostar. From this castle, Sebeneco is distant two hundred miles, and between them on the river Mostar is Ghabla, a harbour which has its Capudan. On the opposite side are two long islands belonging to the Venetians which are called Braj (Brazza), and Lesina. Beyond Ghabla is Ispalat (Spalatra), which also belongs to the Venetians, and is a well-known port and harbour. Near that, on an elevated spot on the land, is Kelis, a strong citadel, which has lately been taken by the Venetians; but means must be used to recover it. Beyond this, on the coast, is Shebenic (Sebenico), a strong castle, with a spacious harbour, into which falls a great river that flows from the north. Near this castle is a rocky eminence where Tekeli Pasha was once routed. Zadra (Zara), twenty miles beyond Sebenico, is a strong fortress, almost entirely surrounded by the sea, being only on one side slightly connected with the land.   Between these two castles, at the place where the river Darmah falls into the sea, is the fort of Iskaradin.   The above river divides the districts of Kerka and Kelis, all the forts of which have been taken by the Venetians.   Here the Bosnia shore terminates.

DESCRIPTION OF THE CHRISTIAN TOWNS.

Along the coast beyond Zara are the forts of Nodi and Sein (Zeng), belonging to the Germans.   Behind them, on the land, are Abrutisa, Bahka, Todornoi, Bamaluka, and Kostanitza.   These are the frontiers of Croatia.   Then, between Zara and Venice, which is a space of one hundred and fifty miles, lies the country of Istria.   It is in the form of a square, and three sides of it are surrounded by the sea.   It has in it, and on the shores, many towns and forts, some of which are governed by the Venetians, and some by the German princes. Farther on is the district of Friuli, called also Forum Julii, which signifies the market of Julius Cæsar.   It is a very large district, and part of it borders on the city of Venice.   The sources of the rivers Save and Drave are in it, and it contains numerous towns and forts, most of which are governed by the Venetians, though they are all tributary to the Emperor (of Germany).   In travelling to Venice we go through this country.   All its towns and forts are marked in my translation of the Atlas Minor.

VENICE.

Venedik, as described in the Atlas, has various significations : it is also called Venechia and Venetia.   It is a large city, built upon sixty small islands in a corner of the sea like a lake.   Its waters ebb and flow every six hours; and some of the isles are raised like ramparts to prevent the water from overflowing.   This city has three or four passages to the sea ; and although it is not guarded by walls and towers, its being so completely surrounded by water renders it quite safe and free from all danger.   Between the houses there are roads and passages by which passengers and boats may pass from house to house.   Over these waters there are about four hundred and fifty bridges, both of stone and wood.   The largest of these roads they call a canal ; it divides the city into two parts, and over it there is a wonderful bridge.   Eight thousand vessels are constantly in motion, some of which are ornamented with covers, and these they call gondolas. The circumference of the city is nearly eight miles ; and its principal streets are sixty-four in number.   The public and private buildings are excessively grand

and ornamental, especially the church dedicated to the Four Evangelists, which is called St. Marco, and is an astonishing building. It is adorned with the most valuable and expensive stones, and its interior is gilt with pure gold. In the treasury, which they say is a sacred deposit, there are kept the most costly and precious articles; and affirming that the city with all its castles and ships belongs to it, the priests have shackled these fools, and by this artifice have brought under their power all the Christians, small and great. The city has three fine market-places, all adjoining each other : in the square of the principal one is the above-mentioned church; and close to the quay there are two massy columns; upon one of which is set up the standard of St. Marco, and upon the other the image of St. Theodorus. On the flag is represented a lion with wings; by which, and on their coins also, they celebrate the valour of St. Marco, who is said to have been a brave and valiant person. The space between the two columns is the Hall of Justice. The centre of the city they call the Arsenal; which has a spacious building, and being two miles in circumference, it forms a strong castle. Here naval armaments and cannons are daily manufactured and repaired; and the wrecks of fleets, the arms taken from pirates, old vessels, and colours, being deposited in this place, are exhibited to visitors.

The population of Venice is estimated to be three hundred thousand, and it is divided into three classes. Those of the first are called Patricii, and correspond to our *Meshaiékh*. To these belong the management of the state, and the affairs of government. Their principal is called *Doge*, which signifies Duke. He enters into all questions of law, but has not power to act until he has the voice of the people. Amongst the Christians a Duke corresponds to the *Begler Beg* of the Mussulmans, except that the former has his own coin. Those constituting the second order are called *Istadinū*,* and to them are committed civil affairs, customs, and education. The third class is composed of merchants and artisans. In former times the power of this people was vested in a consul, but in the year 555 from the birth of Christ (upon whom be peace!) it was committed to a tribune or chief of a tribe; and this government continued two hundred and fifty-two years, till, in A. D. 707, it became a dukedom: so that from the commencement of the dukedom to the time of the writing of this book, which is A. H. 1067 (A. D. 1656), is a period of nine hundred and fifty years. To proceed : Mer-cator, the author of the Atlas, describing this city, speaks very highly of it, and says that it is the most celebrated city in the world; and being the common port of the universe, merchants of all sorts, and from the most distant countries, trade in it. The number of its inhabitants, and the extent of their wealth, are beyond

* Probably Citadini.

B

conception. On this account the Christians call it the Paradise of the Earth: for although during a period of one thousand years it suffered much, yet it never was under a foreign power. For this reason the Venetians represent their city by the figure of a virgin holding a sword; and this figure they place in all their offices: for they state that her still holding the sword, signifies her having continued a virgin down to the present time. The above-mentioned book, which is an European work, in describing this city, gives the following statement: " that the first founding of Venice was, according to several historians, in A. D. 421, when the inhabitants of Patavia, being attacked by the Hungarians, left that town, and settling on these islands, commenced the building of Venice." Several rivers from the territory of Lombardy fall into the Gulf near it; and the greatest part of the provisions consumed in the city are brought down these rivers. Here terminates the description as given in European books; but Piri Reis in his Bahria says, that ships bound for Venice first touch at Parenza, which is a fort in the territory of Istria, and distant about one hundred miles from Venice. They cannot proceed without a pilot on account of the shallows; they therefore engage one to conduct them from this place. They then proceed till they come in sight of Iskandil and Marco-chaklik: the latter is a high castle, which appears first, and then when they can see the city they cast anchor. Soon after another pilot comes from the city with a small boat, which takes the vessel in tow; and thus they proceed to the harbour. It is forbidden to pilot foreign vessels. The quays are always kept open on account of the tides. In the city there are also water-boats; these they fill with water, and going about the streets they sell it by measure. Fish is plentiful here. The fishermen have boats like skimmers, in which they keep the fish alive; and carrying them through the streets, sell them. On the east side of the city is an island, which they call Muran, where crystal vessels and other glass articles are manufactured.

THE ITALIAN, FRENCH, AND SPANISH COASTS.

Having passed the city of Venice, we come to Ancona, Bashtia, Manfredonia, Brindisi, Cape Otranto, and Cape St. Maria, where the Gulf of Venice terminates. Turning thence to the west, we pass Taranto, Rossano, Cape Cotrone, Spartivento, and Cape Reggio: opposite which, in the island of Chichlia (Sicily), is Cape Messina; and the space between forms the Strait of Messina, which, like the Strait of Constantinople, is very narrow. Beyond these are Naples, Cape Gaeta, the river Rooma (Tiber), upon which a little farther in the land is the city (of Rome), Pantan, Leghorn, which is in the district of Florence, an independent dukedom bordering on the pope's dominions. Farther on is the state of Genoa, which is also an independent government, bordering on Milan. In the French dominions are, Savona, Nice, Afwamort, and Marseilles. Per- pignan, Davina, Barcelona, Tortosa, Cape Carthagena, Malaga,and Jabl-al-Fat'h (Gibraltar), on the Strait of Sabta, are on the Spanish coast. In the Atlas they are called Catalonia, Aragonia, Valencia, and Andalusia. According to compu- tations in several histories, the Rumelian and European coasts are reckoned to be 8047 miles in length ; and the Anatolian, Arabian, and western coasts, 5010 miles : in all 13,057 miles. The principal islands are Sardinia, Corsica, Minorca, Miorca, Ivica, Malta, Crete (or Candia), Cyprus, and Rhodes. In former times all these, except Rhodes, were captured ; and how this was done, I have fully explained in my works called the Fezliket Tarikh and the Jehan Nemah. At present they are all, except Cyprus and Rhodes, in the possession of the Infidels ; and even the subjugation of Candia has not yet been fully accom- plished. God grant that it may soon be effected ! Here our Introduction ends : we shall now proceed to our First Part.

PART FIRST.

Concerning the ancient fleets, victories, and naval wars; accounts of which have, for the sake of example, been arranged and collected from historical books. This Part consists of several Chapters.

CHAPTER I.

Of the Ottoman Capudans, and the expeditions and battles of several Sultans and Admirals, to the time of Kheir al Deen Pasha.

Be it known that before the time of the late illustrious and victorious Sultan Mohammed, the Ottomans had not ventured to undertake naval expeditions, or to engage with the European nations. It is indeed related that in the time of Sultan Murad the Second, they occasionally made excursions to the neighbouring shores and islands; but these expeditions are not worth enumerating. After the taking of Constantinople, when they spread their conquests over land and sea, it became necessary to build ships and make armaments, in order to subdue the fortresses and castles on the Rumelian and Anatolian shores, and in the islands of the Mediterranean.

When they first besieged Constantinople on the land side, and saw the little success they had, they found the necessity of raising a proper fleet in order to attack the city by sea; and to the management of this affair, Soleiman Beg, son of Balta, was appointed. According to one account he built the vessels behind Sūdlūja; but, according to the Tāj al Tuarikh, behind the castle of Rumeili.

This Soleiman Beg then, it appears, was the first Capudan of this nation, for before the capture of Constantinople no mention is made in any history of the harbour of Gallipoli, or its capudan, whereas there is at present, near that castle, a port named after this Soleiman Beg.

It is related in the above-mentioned work, that a chain being drawn across the bay which separates Galata from Constantinople, it was found utterly impossible to bring up the vessels to attack the city on that side; but orders being given to move from Galata, they conducted the ships to Iengi Hissar, where, by a novel and surprising contrivance of raising weights, they lifted them out of the water, and placing them on oiled rollers, thus carried them over the land, and again lowered them into the sea. These vessels were filled with the most valiant warriors; and parapets being erected, they fought bravely, completely discomfited the Infidels, and at last vanquished the city.

The various expeditions that succeeded this distinguished victory, and the account of their leaders, shall now follow in order.

THE EXPEDITION TO ENOS.

Soon after the capture of Constantinople, the cazy and inhabitants of Ferra having represented that they were much annoyed by the wickedness of the Infidels of Enos, his Majesty (Sultan Mohammed) instantly resolved on subjugating those rebels; in consequence of which, Khass Ionas was summoned to the Sublime Porte, and his Majesty having communicated his design, ordered him to collect all the troops that were at hand; to fit out ten triremes, and sail with all possible haste to the appointed place. He further charged him not to disclose the place of their destination to any one, till they reached it; whilst he himself would lead on his victorious army by land. Ionas Beg, in conformity with his instructions, put out to sea, and with favourable winds, in a short time arrived at the castle, to which he laid siege. The imperial banners of victory, being equally expeditious, were also raised; and the Infidels, being filled with terror, offered stipulations, and surrendered the fortress. Ionas Beg after this, by the sultan's command, attacked another castle on the island of Tashūz (Tasse), opposite Enos, which he reduced, and returned.

THE EXPEDITION TO AMASSERO, SINOPE, AND TREBISOND.

In the year of the Hejra 864 (A. D. 1459), the victorious sultan, Mohammed Khan, proceeded by land to reduce Amassero, a castle on the shores of the Black Sea; and at the same time sent forward other forces by sea. Being again crowned with success, he turned his attention to Sinope, then occupied by Ismael Beg, son of Isfendiar; and the grand vizier, Mohammed Pasha, having fitted up a fleet of one hundred vessels, manned by warlike heroes, set sail, and on his way to Trebisond touched at Sinope, where the land forces having also arrived, they besieged the castle both by sea and land. The helpless Emir Ismael surrendered without resistance, and delivered the castle to the Sublime Porte. Having, besides this, subjugated Kastamouni, the victorious fleet proceeded towards Sinope, whither the imperial forces also marched; and after a short siege, the enemy stipulated, and surrendered the city.

In the European history, which I translated from the Latin into Turkish, I have mentioned that at this time Ismael Beg built a very large ship of nine hundred tons. This vessel the Emperor sent to Constantinople. About the same time Alfonso, the king of Aragonia, built a vessel which held four thousand tons; and soon after built two others, which in point of size had never been equalled, but they could not use them; and striking against each other in the harbour, they were dashed to pieces.

The Venetians also at this period, having made peace with the Genoese, began to build immense vessels. Sultan Mahommed at the same time built one of three thousand tons, but, as they were launching it, it sunk in the harbour, and the builders were obliged to fly. *Ton (fouchi)* is a phrase peculiar to ships of the ocean, and is used to designate their size.

THE EXPEDITION TO METYLINI.

In the year of the Hejra 866 (A. D. 1461), the emperor having returned from an expedition to Wallachia, he made preparations for the capture of Meddeli (Metylini); for which purpose he proceeded to the neighbourhood of Gallipoli, and there gave orders for the preparing of the fleet. When the Constantinople ships had also arrived, they set sail; whilst his Majesty, with the Imperial and Anatolian troops, having passed the Strait at Gallipoli, proceeded to Ayazmend; and the ships, tall as mountains, anchored opposite Metylini. When the forces were about to commence an attack, the governor of the island came out, offered stipulations, and surrendered the garrison. His private property they returned to him, and sent him to his own country. Having established laws, and divided the island, they left the natives as subjects, registered the houses, and returned.

THE EXPEDITION TO THE NEGROPONT.

In the year 872 (A. D. 1467), the army having returned from an expedition into Caramania, a complaint was made that the Venetian general with upwards of sixty vessels had made an attack upon Enos; taken prisoners the cazy, the khatib (priest), and several Mussulmans; and had plundered the neighbouring district. In consequence of this, Mahmood Pasha was ordered to proceed to Gallipoli to collect the fleet; and on this occasion all the vessels on the Ottoman coasts were given in charge to him. Among the Greek islands, the Negropont still remained in the hands of the Christians; and from its channel the Mussulmans received much harm; whereas the general, from his avarice, exacted a great revenue from the inhabitants of the island.

In 873, therefore, the victorious forces proceeded both by land and water towards the island; and the pasha having made all preparations for its attack, besieged it with upwards of one hundred ships. The bridges, which had been cut down, were supplied by suspending temporary ones from the vessels, by means of which the soldiers ascended the castle and mounted the battlements. Just at this time the general, with eighty vessels, arrived, to give assistance to the besieged; but when he saw the Mussulman forces, he cast anchor and looked on with despair. His intention was, that whilst the Mussulman vessels were cruising about the island, he also would approach it on one side, and thus prevent its capture; and for this purpose he sent out several caicks to endeavour to take some one from whom they might learn the day of the intended attack. One of the Mahommedan men who had deserted went over to the ships of the Infidels, and being found by the spies was immediately taken before the general, who ascertained from him that the criers had announced that the attack was to take place in three days. The general anxiously waited for that day, and began to make preparations for the combat; but those on the other side having learned that the enemy was informed of their designs, resolved to attack the castle without further delay; and the same night the criers raising their voices to the stars, proclaimed that the morrow should be the day of plunder, and admonished the soldiers to be in readiness. As soon as it was morning, and long before the Infidels had opened their eyes, the soldiers, in the hope of plunder, assaulted the castle, and entered it by the breaches they had

made. Those who were considered fit for service were made captives, and the
rest were killed; whilst the victors were enriched with money and property
beyond compute. In the forenoon the colours hoisted on the tower caught the
eyes of the Infidels, who were so mortified that they spread their sails, and
turned their helms. After this fine fortification was reduced, the victors proceeded to the small fort called Kuzil Hissar, situated on the banks of the island,
and in which the treasury of the Infidels was deposited. This they also subjugated, and the property they found in it they transferred to the royal treasury;
and with cheerfulness of mind returned to the seat of dominion.

THE EXPEDITION TO KAFA AND AZAK.

The territory of Kafa, lying on the shores of the Black Sea, having for many
ages been in the possession of the Genoese, the Turkish and Tartar princes,
though united by their proximity to each other, had never, as yet, on account of
its strong fortifications, been able to reduce it. In 880 (A. D. 1475), the
victorious sultan Mohammed Khan, having resolved upon its subjugation, gave
orders to Keduk Ahmed Pasha to prepare the fleet. The pasha immediately
collected a number of galleys, triremes, &c., amounting in all to three hundred
vessels, and having prepared his Janissaries and Azabs,* kissed his hand, and
according to custom bowed to the princes and nobles; after which he left the
divan, went down to the harbour and embarked. With favourable winds he
arrived in a short time on the shores of Kafa, where he landed and laid siege to
the castle.† The Christians not daring to stand against the arms of the Faithful,
delivered up the castle with stipulations, and left it. The castle being taken,
they proceeded to subjugate its dependencies; and Azak, which is the boundary
of the Sakalaba kingdoms,‡ being also reduced, by proper management they
subjugated all the disaffected. The people of Kafa had their rights restored to
them, and the place became subject to the Ottoman power. The date of this
victory was called A Favour.§

* Azabs are the militia of Turkey.
† The name of the castle is not given, but it is probable it was Kafa.
‡ Sakalaba. The countries to the north of the Black Sea, as Poland, Russia, &c.
§ This is a chronogram. The letters of the word shafakat, a favour, make up the number 880.

THE EXPEDITION TO PUGLIA.

Keduk Ahmed Pasha, having been dismissed from the office of grand vezier and imprisoned, was by some circumstance brought before the Sultan Mohammed Khan on his return from an expedition to Eskenderia. On this occasion the Sultan was pleased to bestow the *sanjak* of Avlona on the pasha. In 884 he came to court, and having represented the facility with which Puglia, a district of Italy opposite Avlona, might be conquered, he petitioned for forces, and accordingly orders were issued to prepare a fleet. The necessary provisions were given him, and having collected a select troop of the bravest men of Roumelia and Anatolia, and some thousands of janissaries and Azabs, the pasha sailed for the coast of Puglia. In his first attack he took the castle of Taranto, and reduced by force of arms several other places in the neighbourhood, in each of which he stationed troops. But the governor of Puglia, an infidel called Raika, represented his case to the king of Spain, who immediately sent assistance to him. Of this the pasha had information, and Sultan Mohammed Khan* dying at that time, he embarked for the Porte under the pretence of paying his respects to the new Sultan. In 886 the infidel, having arrived with forty vessels and an army, retook the whole of the fortresses, and put to the sword most of the troops that were stationed in them. Elated by this success, he resolved on overtaking the pasha, and for this purpose pursued him at sea for some time; but the pasha had reached the Porte in safety.

THE EXPEDITION TO MOTA.

In 884 the illustrious Emperor, returning from a journey to Eskenderia, sent the beg of Koja-eili with thirty *brak kadargas*,† to take Mota, a castle situated on the sea of Azoph, in the neighbourhood of Kaffa, and which still remained in the possession of the infidels. On a former occasion, Keduk Ahmed Pasha, being pressed with more important affairs, did not attempt to take it; but at this time, as soon as it was blockaded by the noble troops, it was surrendered and evacuated by the infidel its governor.

---

* Sultan Mohammed Khan, the conqueror of Constantinople, died at Mal-dipa, A. H. 886, A. D. 1481.

† A species of light-sailing vessels.

C

THE FORTIFYING OF BOOSJA.

The island Boosja (Tenedos), near the Straits (of the Dardanelles), being destitute of a fortress, and as the levend* were in the habit of taking up their quarters there, a royal order was issued the same year, that a fortress should be erected near the shore of the island, and that those who were willing might reside in the neighbourhood exempt from taxes. The island of Lemnos, also, which they call *Lemni*, was fortified about the same time.

THE EXPEDITION TO RHODES.

The Moslems who resided in the island of Rhodes being much molested by the infidels, the chief commander, Vezier Messih Pasha, was in the year 885 ordered to proceed thither with three thousand janissaries and four thousand Azabs. Besides the vessels from Constantinople, sixty others had been built at Gallipoli. With these they set sail, and arrived at the island of Rhodes. They blockaded the castle both by sea and land, but first attacked the tower on the west towards the water, because from this tower the troops had been much annoyed. They made a bridge from the water, so as to reach the tower; but during a fierce attack upon the latter, the bridge, owing to the immense crowd, gave way, and upwards of a thousand men perished in the water. They again took courage, once more made a brave assault upon the castle, and had even raised their standard on the walls, which were covered with troops. These fierce warriors having also whetted the teeth of avarice with the hope of plunder, were rushing on to seize their prey, when Messih Pasha, unwilling that the riches of a fortified place like Rhodes should fall a prey to the soldiery, gave orders that as the treasury of the place belonged exclusively to the Sultan, no one should dare to touch it. As soon as this unwelcome intelligence was spread amongst the soldiers, those on the outside would proceed no farther, whilst those in the interior remained motionless; and the enemy, having made a violent rush from one quarter, put to the sword all they met. Soleiman Pasha Beg of Costamoni likewise shared the fate of martyrdom. Thus the avarice of Messih Pasha and the selfishness of the troops were the cause of this ill fortune. At last he withdrew from the castle, and amidst loud complaints directed his course towards the capital. On his way he attacked the castle of Bodrun; but being

---

* Levend ; a sort of volunteers who serve in the Turkish navy.

unsuccessful here also, he returned to the Porte. When he landed at Beshektash the sanjak of Gallipoli was given to him, and to this district he immediately
proceeded.

THE EXPEDITION TO AVLONA.

In the year 889 the Sultan Bayezid Khan, having sent forward his fleet by
the Black sea and proceeded thither himself by land, completely reduced Kili *
and Ak-Kerman.   In 897 the beg of Semendreh sent information that the
king of Hungary being dead, the governor of Belgrade had promised allegiance
to the Sultan. In consequence of this message his majesty directed his course
to that quarter ; but fearing it might only be a false promise, and that he might
not return empty handed, he gave orders to Gubegu Senan Pasha to sail for
Avlona with three hundred vessels ; so that in case he should not succeed in the
capture of Belgrade, he might as it were turn his forces to that quarter, and
plunder the Arnaout shores. When the preparations for the expedition were
completed, and his majesty was marching towards Sofia, the new king sent an
apology and asked forgiveness : he therefore turned towards the Arnaout shores,
and passed on by Monaster to Dipa-diln, whilst Davud Pasha laid waste a great
part of that district and returned. The fleet also attacked several places along
the coasts, and plundered the rebels.

THE EXPEDITION TO LEPANTO.

The Sultan Bayezid Khan, contemplating an expedition in order to subdue the
districts of the Morea and Enabekht (Lepanto), began about this time to build
large ships. He appointed Davud Pasha, then a capudan, his ser-asker (com-
mander-in-chief). He built two immense *kokas*, the length of each being seventy
cubits and the breadth thirty cubits. The masts were of several trees joined
together, and in the middle measured four cubits in circumference. The maintop
was capable of holding forty men in armour, who might thence discharge their
arrows and muskets. The builders and other labourers employed were servants
of the Sultan ; and the building materials being all the productions of the Ottoman empire, were valued at twenty thousand florins. According to the state-
ments of several respectable historians, the builder of these vessels was one

* Kili, the ancient Lycostomos, a town on the northern mouth of the Danube.

Iani, who having seen ship-building at Venice, had there learned the art. These vessels had two decks, the one like that of a galleon, and the other like that of a *mavuna (trireme)*; and on the side of each of these, according to custom, were two port-holes, in which immense guns were placed. Along the upper deck was a netting, under which on both sides were four-and-twenty oars, each pulled by nine men. The sterns were like those of a galleon, and from them boats were suspended. Each of these ships contained two thousand soldiers and sailors. The command of the one was given to Kemal Reis, and that of the other to Brak Reis. The whole fleet consisted of three hundred vessels of various sorts; and these being filled with the most intrepid warriors, were sent towards Enabekht. The illustrious Emperor also, about the end of the month Sheval, in the year 904, (A.D. 1498,) leaving Constantinople, proceeded to Adrianople, and sent Mustaffa Pasha, the begler-beg of Roumelia, to besiege Enabekht. When the pasha arrived at this place, the infidel who had charge of it sent out a message to say he was ordered not to give up the garrison until the Moslem fleet had entered the gulf of Lepanto. Upon this Mustaffa Pasha turned aside into the country to wait the arrival of the fleet, which by contrary winds had been kept at sea for three months. At last, when they touched on the shores of the Morea, another contrary gale arose, and with difficulty they made into the harbour of an island opposite Motone, in which they remained twenty days. After this they began to be pressed by the failure of their provisions and water: when they attempted to go on shore the infidels prevented them, and on the other side they were continually harassed by the enemy's ships. At last the beg of the Morea, Khalil Pasha, made known their situation by sending a courier to the Sultan Bayezid Khan, who at that time had arrived at the plain of Chatalaja, in the vicinity of Enabekht. The Sultan immediately issued orders that Hersek Oghli Ahmed Pasha with the Anatolian forces should enter the Morea and render assistance to the fleet. Ahmed Pasha accordingly set out with haste, but before he reached Motone they had left the harbour, and were on their way to Navarin. The pasha soon after joined the vessels at Helomej.

The royal fleet having passed Navarin and arrived at Brak island, were again met by the abject infidels, who sailed directly against them. On a former occasion the enemy had been much annoyed by Kemal Reis, and now the enmity in their breasts was without bounds. The beg of Jeni-sheher, Kemal Beg, being on board the vessel of Brak Reis, they supposed it to be that of Kemal Reis, attacked it furiously, and many on both sides fell into the whirl-pool of destruction. Two *kokas*, each containing a thousand men, and a trireme and barge with five hundred men, succeeded in placing the vessel of Brak Reis in the centre; but in this position, the two smaller vessels not being able to sustain the fire of Brak Reis, they both sunk, and most of the infidels on board were drowned; a few were however taken up by hooks into the other boats and made prisoners. The two *kokas* then bore down on Brak Reis, and the engagement being extended, Brak Reis threw burning pitch into them, and thus burnt up the rascals with their ships. But all his exertions to detach his own vessel were fruitless, and at last that also caught fire. Kemal Beg, Brak Reis, and Kara Hassan, with about five hundred brave men, perished by this catastrophe. The other heroes who fell into the sea were taken up into boats, by which means about seven hundred were saved. The two *kokas* were also burnt, and of those that were swimming, besides the drowned and burnt, seven hundred of the enemy were killed. A galleon which had come to their assistance was also taken, and the infidels on board were made prisoners. The island near which this engagement took place was hence called *Brak-atasi* (the island of Brak).

After this, one hundred and fifty Venetian vessels having shut up the entrance of the gulf of Lepanto, and cannons being placed at the mouth of it, the commanders stood prepared for an engagement. The Moslem ships then came up, and in attempting to enter the gulf received the enemy's fire. Here also a fierce engagement took place, and several brave men fell. At last the Divine Ruler favoured the armies of Islamism, so that they completely destroyed the enemy's fleet. In short, in the neighbourhood of Motone, after they had left the harbour, at the island of Brak, and on their entering the gulf of Lepanto, they had sharp battles with the enemy. At length they passed the strait, and proceeded towards Lepanto, notwithstanding the great number of cannons and ships, and although the current was against them. When they reached the fortress the heroes went out to blockade it; but the besieged, according to their former promise, sent out the keys to Mustaffa Pasha, and in the following year evacuated it. The capture of the fortress being reported to his majesty, Ahmed Pasha left his ship, and the royal fleet was ordered to winter in the liman of Amar Beg, near Kirma. His majesty then returned to Adrianople.

THE EXPEDITION TO MOTONE AND CORONE.

Although the greater part of the Morea had been subjugated in the time of Abul-Fat'h (Mohammed II.), the fortresses of Motone and Corone on the coast still remained in the hands of the infidels. For the subjugation of these, the beg of Prevesa, Mustaffa Beg, was directed to prepare before the approaching spring forty vessels, which were to be added to the fleet. During the summer

he built twenty vessels, and was just finishing them, when one dark night the
infidels came and set fire to them all.   Mustaffa Beg now began to finish the
other vessels, and about this time the combination of the infidel tribes to attack
the Ottoman territory by sea was made known to the Sublime Porte; in consequence of which Iacub Pasha, and several noble begs, with ten thousand
infantry and twenty thousand cavalry, were sent to assist in repairing the fleet
then wintering at Enabekht, whence they had orders to sail with the fleet in
the spring for Motone.   The Khoonkar * also, in the month of Ramazan 905,†
(A.D. 1499) left Adrianople and proceeded to the Morea.   When the arrival
of Iacub Pasha and his fleet at Motone was announced to his majesty, after
having rested twenty days at Londar, he proceeded to the neighbourhood of the
castle of Motone.   The troops then surrounded the castle by land and sea, and
with their cannon rased its walls to the ground.   They were on the point of
taking it when the enemy's fleet arrived, and made preparations for an engagement.   The Moslem troops took two of the enemy's ships, and punished the
infidels found in them opposite the castle.   They also sunk one of their
triremes, and burnt several of their other ships.   While they were thus on the
point of victory, four galleys arrived from Venice, carrying ammunition, and
some thousands of artillery-men, passed through the fleet at a time when the
Moslems were off their guard, and as soon as they had landed their cargo
within the castle, set fire to the four galleys.   This being reported to the Sultan,
his majesty in a rage gave orders that as soon as the enemy began to remove
the ammunition that had been taken in, they should make a general attack.
Upon this Senan Pasha, the begler-beg of Anatolia, entered the castle by a
ladder, through a breach which he had made, and the whole army attacking it
furiously, they continued to fight from mid-day till sun-set in a manner that
baffles description.   At this time fire broke out in the castle, and the infidels
being terrified, the Moslems took possession of the castle and put the enemy to
the sword.   This victory happened on the fourteenth of Moharrem 906.

For the subjugation of Corone Ali Pasha was sent by land, and the capudan
with his fleet by sea.   Ali Pasha having announced his intention of besieging
Navarin, the inhabitants gave up the castle on condition that they should be
permitted to go out of it.   When the troops arrived at Corone, the inhabitants
of that place also surrendered, and with their families and property departed to
Frankestan.

---

* One of the Sultan's titles.

† In the original the date is 970 ; but this is evidently a mistake, as may be seen below ; or by consulting the author's chronological tables.

The Sultan having returned to the capital, Ali Pasha turned his attention to the capture of Astaffa; but in the mean time the infidels, by some means or other, retook the castle of Navarin. When the pasha was informed of this, he reported it to the Divan, and immediately returned to Navarin. He also sent thither Kemal Reis with thirty vessels. When they arrived at the castle they attacked the fleet lying in the harbour, and in their first attack took eight of the enemy's ships, and killed the infidels that were in them. Several brave men who had come with the pasha then scaled the walls, bound the chiefs, and made about three thousand infidels food for the sword.

THE EXPEDITION TO MITYLENE.

The Venetians, in order to revenge themselves for the loss of Enabekht, Motone and Corone, sent to beg assistance from the king of France,* who, having equipped some vessels and appointed his nephew commander, sent them to join the Venetian fleet. The whole, amounting to two hundred vessels, set sail, and in the month of Rabia-al-Avul 907 (A.D. 1501) came upon Mity-lene. The Prince Korkud, being informed of this, sent one of his agas with eight hundred men to Ayazmend, whence one dark night they sailed for Mity-lene, and with the assistance of Krassi Beg and his troops, massacring the infidel tribes, they entered the castle; in doing which the aga was killed. When this unpleasant news reached the Sultan, his majesty without loss of time filled the vessels that were at hand with troops, of which Hersek Oghli Ahmed Pasha was commander; and Senan Pasha, the governor of Anatolia, was also ordered to join the fleet with the forces of his district. When Ahmed Pasha arrived in the neighbourhood of Mitylene the infidels had blockaded the castle ; but as the French general was about to enter it he was killed; and all the troops that had been stationed about the castle seeing this betook themselves to flight. The Venetians also took refuge in their ships and went off. The pro-tection of the fortress being left to the begler-beg of Anatolia, Ahmed Pasha returned to the Porte.

This Ahmed Pasha, after being made grand vezier, was dismissed. In 912 he was made a capudan, which office he held for five years, and in 917 he again became grand vezier.

It is recorded that this expedition gave rise to the levying of taxes and enlist-

---

* Cantemir in giving an account of this expedition doubts whether it was the king of France who assisted the Venetians on this occasion, because the Turks call all the European nations Franks ; but our author generally distinguishes France by the name of *Fransa*.

ing galley-men. Formerly these impositions were not made on the subjects ; but from that time to the present they have been authorised by law, and are raised annually.

As the Venetian and Moslem fleets did not come to an engagement, after the former were driven from Mitylene, the necessity of silence and of refraining from their intended revenge, on their part, and various causes on the part of the latter, induced them to consider an armistice desirable. After this no attacks were made on any of their districts either by land or sea, and the fleet was employed only in protecting the Ottoman dominions. When however the power of the Persian kings in the East began to increase, the disturbances of the *Rafezis*,* and the retirement of Sultan Bayezid Khan on account of his great age, produced negligence in the ministers, and tended to injure the prosperity of the state ; and Sultan Selim, after his ascension to the throne, being occupied in matters that demanded immediate attention,—in punishing the Persians,† and subjugating the countries of Egypt and Syria,—the possessions of the infidels thus remained unmolested. The Venetians and Hungarians also, duly appreciating this peace, did not make the least stir. On the decease of Sultan Selim, Soleiman Khan coming to the throne, began to subjugate all those places which he thought proper should be annexed to the Ottoman dominions ; and opening both by land and sea the gates of war, he terminated that armistice which from necessity had been adopted during the reign of his illustrious father, and in his second expedition succeeded in the capture of Rhodes.

PREPARATION OF A FLEET FOR RHODES.

In the year 923 (A. D. 1517), during the reign of Sultan Selim the First, the countries of Egypt having been subdued and added to the Ottoman dominions, in 925 it was considered necessary to open a road for the importation of the productions of that country. For this purpose the capture of Rhodes, the seat of pirates, was suggested to the victorious Sultan, who immediately began to prepare a fleet ; but although for a long time reports of an intended expedition were heard from the ministers and nobles, yet from the movements of the Sultan nothing to that effect could be perceived, till one day with his nobles and attend-

---

* *Rafezi*, the Mohammedan sect of the Shiites, or followers of Ali, which chiefly prevails in Persia. The Turks consider them heretics.

† In the original *surkh ser*, red heads, a term of contempt applied by the Turks to the Persians.

ants he went out to visit the tomb of Abi Aiub Ansari, and standing on his usual spot beside the high dome near his nurse's tomb, he read the *Fatihat*.* Looking towards the channel, he saw one of the newly built vessels cruising about, and in a rage demanded to know by whose authority they had put it to sea, before an expedition had been determined upon ; at the same time giving orders for the execution of the Capudan Jafar Aga. Piri Pasha with some difficulty satisfied him, by saying that the vessel had been put to sea merely to try it. On his majesty's return he severely reprimanded the veziers, saying, "Whilst I am accustomed to subdue kingdoms, you waste the means in taking a single castle, the requisite for which is ammunition. How many months will your ammunition last? and are the necessary stores in readiness ?" The veziers informed him of what stores they had, but declined giving any account of their ammunition till the next day, and thus they departed with many reproaches. The next morning they reported to his majesty that their ammunition was sufficient for four months. His majesty in a scornful manner replied, that whilst his grandfather Sultan Mohammed Khan's disgrace with respect to Rhodes was not yet forgotten, they wished to double it on him, especially as four months' ammunition was by no means sufficient for the reduction of a fortress like Rhodes, which, if it were taken in double that time, would be highly creditable : that he was determined to undertake no expedition on such vain counsel, nor by the advice of any one ; and concluded by saying, that for himself he had no voyage in view, except the one to eternity. According to his prediction, the fortress was with difficulty taken in the time he specified ; and about six months after this conversation he departed to the world of spirits.

THE EXPEDITION TO RHODES.

Sultan Soleiman Khan, of happy memory, ascended the throne in 926 (A. D. 1519); and the violence and oppression of Capudan Jafar Beg having been discovered, he was hanged, and his office was given to Iilak Mustaffa Pasha. After the capture of Belgrade, the subjugation of Rhodes being considered most important, the emperor, in the month of Rajab 928, came to the capital and issued orders for the preparation of an immense fleet ; and a great number of sailors and azabs being collected, the second vezier, Mustaffa Pasha, was appointed commander. On an auspicious day they set out, and with about seven

* The first chapter of the Koran.

D

hundred vessels of various sorts sailed for the Mediterranean. The Capudan Pasha also joined them with the ships he had prepared at Gallipoli; and in the month of Rajab 928 the illustrious emperor passed over to Skutari, whence he pursued his journey by land. The Roumeili troops, having marched by different routes, joined the royal camp in the vales of Moghala; and on the third of Rajab his majesty crossed over to a small island opposite Marmaross. Previously to this, the fleet having arrived in the vicinity of Rhodes, the commander, Kara Mahmūd Reis, sent a few vessels to an island called Herka, and reduced its fortress. After this the fleet touched opposite Jem-Baghche. The heavy vessels were stationed to guard the channel; whilst the pasha, with three hundred galleys, proceeded to the fortress of Rhodes, and entered the harbour of Cape Oghuz. Having arranged their cannon, on the fifth of Ramazan they blockaded the fortress: a week after, Bali Beg, one of the Egyptian begs, arrived, and with twenty-four galleys, which had sailed before him, brought additional ammunition and stores. They continued to have sharp battles, and to make brave assaults, till the end of *Sheval;* and the *Arab* tower being the occasion of much molestation to the troops, orders were given to attack it. In doing this, although they succeeded in passing the trench, and raised their flag on the walls and towers, yet the enemy bore down and repelled them; and Bâli Beg, the beg of Seké, and Ali Beg, the beg of Avlona, fell as martyrs. As they could not thus effect any thing, they began, with the approbation of the experienced among them to raise a mound, and after five months of continued warfare they raised it to a level with the walls. The infidels within the castle, helpless and confounded, and not being able to screen themselves from the cannons and muskets, on the fifth of Seffer 929, they surrendered the fortress. Its governor, Mighali Masturi,* was permitted to go out, and accordingly he went over to Malta. The islands subject to Rhodes, such as Takhtalu, Londas, Istanco, and Bodrum, being also subdued and all necessary arrangements completed, the victorious emperor, on the fourteenth of the same month, with honor and dignity proceeded to Mantesha, whence by hasty marches he returned to the capital.

THE EXPEDITION OF SALMAN REIS.

Before this period the Ottoman Sultans had not sent their victorious arms to the Indian Ocean. In the year 932, (A. D. 1525,) the Sultan Soleiman appointed the Corsair Salman Reis a capudan and commander, and sent him with

_____
* The Grand-master.

twenty galleys to that quarter. He proceeded along the coasts of Aden and Yemen, and plundered the habitations of the rebellious and such as were not well affected to the Porte ; in consequence of which, the sheikhs and Arabs of those districts came out to him with numerous presents, offered their services, and bound themselves to transmit their taxes.

THE EXPEDITION OF KEMAN-KESH.

About this time the office of capudan was held by Keman-Kesh Ahmed Beg, who in 940 sailed with eighty galleys, on an expedition to the Mediterranean, and having pillaged several of the infidel's coasts, returned and was employed in the royal arsenal. This capudan was famous for his great strength, for he could hold an enraged ram with one hand. He was also a good archer.* He held the office of capudan till the arrival of Khair-ad-din Pasha from Algiers, about which time he died.

* His name *Keman-Kesh* signifies an archer.

CHAPTER II.

Respecting the Affairs of Khair-ad-din Pasha.

THIS pasha, who arrived at the highest honours of his country, was a brave and valiant soldier, and altogether an astonishing person. When he was brought before the Sultan Soleiman Khan, he was treated with the greatest attention, and was requested to write an account of his adventures. In compliance with this request he selected, from the writings of those who had been with him, accounts of his principal adventures; and having formed them into a book, he forwarded it to the Sultan of happy memory.

The greater part of these adventures we have extracted from that work, and shall here insert them in order.

The pasha's name was Hezr. His father Iacub was a soldier's son at Aja Ava, and at the capture of Metylini enlisted in the volunteers, and remained in that island. He had four sons, Is'hak, Oruj, Hezr, and Elias, each of whom carried on a trade at sea. Is'hak afterwards settled at Metylini; Oruj continued his voyages to Egypt and Trabalos Sham; and Hezr to Saros and Salonica. Whilst Oruj and his brother Elias were sailing to Trabalos, they were attacked by some infidels of Rhodes, and Elias fell in the struggle. Hezr was also made a prisoner, and remained some time in the island. When he regained his liberty, he petitioned Sultan Corcud, who was then in Anatolia, for permission to go out as a corsair; which being granted, he sailed with a galley of eighteen benches. He first plundered the infidels' ships about Rhodes, and then passed over to the coasts of Italy, where he attacked some boats, and after several engagements, in which he took considerable booty, returned and wintered at Eskenderia. Thence he went to the island of Jarba, where he left his cargo, and made preparations for a voyage to the infidel countries. On the accession of Sultan Selim to the throne, his brother, Corcud Khan, was obliged to conceal himself,

and the Mediterranean ships were prohibited from sailing. Khair-ad-din therefore took ship at Metylini, and sailed to Maghreb; whilst his brother Oruj
proceeded to the island of Jarba. Here the two brothers met, and formed an
agreement to carry on their wars together; after which they repaired to Tunis,
and requested some place of abode from the governor. At that time Tunis was
held by Beni Hefs, who appointed for their use the castle of Halk-al-vad, upon
condition that he should receive a fifth part of all their plunder.

THE ENGAGEMENTS OF ORUJ AND KHAIR-AD-DIN.

After the winter had passed, and the season for sailing had returned, the two
corsairs fitted up two vessels, and left Halk-al-vad. They first came in contact
with a large Genoese vessel, with a cargo of corn, which they seized without any
ceremony. Shortly afterwards they met a huge merchant ship laden with cloth:
this they also took without any loss of time; and returned to Tunis, where they
gave up a fifth part of their plunder, and divided the remainder. They then once
more made for the infidel coasts, and soon met a Spanish vessel in full sail, to
which they made up; but there being on board of her an infidel beg, they had
to fight sharply for some time. At last however they took the ship.

The fame of these two men now began to be very conspicuous, and their valour
was celebrated along the shores of the Mediterranean. On one occasion they
went out with four ships, and proceeded to a castle called Bajaia (Bujia), in
the vicinity of Trabalos (Tripoli), of which they had obtained possession. Here
they were opposed by the Spanish fleet, which gave them battle; but they
bravely resisted them, and by the favour of God were victorious. They took two
of the ships, and dispersed the rest, except one which Oruj Reis sunk. After
the engagement Oruj Reis went out, and whilst he was surveying the castle, the
enemy made an attempt to recover their vessels. Whilst Oruj Reis was employed
in repelling them, a shot from the castle wounded his left arm. His brother
took him on board, and had his arm dressed; but, as the wound seemed incurable,
they were obliged to amputate it. In the mean time they took a barge and
several small vessels, which they sent to Tunis. Khair-ad-din himself sailed to
the island of Majorca, which he attacked, reduced several of the fortresses,
and enriched himself with the plunder of the villages. Whilst he continued
his cruise, the capudan of Corsica came out with eight galleys, and made preparations for an engagement. Khair-ad-din turned upon the capudan's galley
and attacked it; but the contest was long, and many men fell on both sides. At
last the infidels were beaten, and began to retreat. The two vessels which they

had taken Khair-ad-din obliged them to give up.   He then returned to Tunis, where he left Oruj Reis on account of his wound.

THE ENGAGEMENTS OF KHAIR-AD-DIN.

During the winter the warrior again went to sea, and became exceedingly rich, having taken in one month three thousand eight hundred prisoners and twenty ships.   The captives he retained for himself, but all the booty he divided among his men.   In the spring he again took the command of seven private vessels, and went to sea.   On this occasion he attacked a town on the infidel coast, and having taken about one thousand eight hundred prisoners, he sold them for two thousand florins, and returned.   Whilst his vessels were dispersed in search of plunder, one night after he had lighted his lantern, he was followed by four barges, which he did not observe till the next morning, when he turned upon them and took all the four.   These were laden with cloth;   and when he carried them to Tunis, he took out of them eight thousand pastas and bales of cloth.   Previously to this, on the same night, he had given chase to another barge, which however contrived to escape from him, but it was taken by the other ships, and being a French vessel, and fully laden, he entrusted it to his nephew, Mohi-ad-din Reis, and sent it with presents to the Porte;   in return for which, the Porte sent him two galleys and a robe of honour.   After this no ship could venture to withstand Khair-ad-din.

THE EXPEDITION TO BEJAIA AND THE CAPTURE OF SHARSHAL.

The warrior and his brother once more prepared ten vessels, and went out on an expedition to Bajaia.   On their way they attacked a small fortress called Sharshal or Jajl, which they took without any difficulty;   and putting into chains a hundred infidels whom they found in it, they left three ships with fifty men to guard it.

After this they went on to the castle of Bajaia, where they landed their men and took out their cannon.   Having closely blockaded it, they took it by assault on the fourth day.   Besides those who fell, they took five thousand prisoners;   and the plunder of the castle they allotted to the twenty thousand Arabs who had come to their assistance.   They then laid siege to the second castle, which they surrounded for twenty days;   but at last, their ammunition falling short, they sent for assistance to the Sultan of Tunis, who however denied it them.   In the mean time, an infidel fleet of two hundred vessels arrived, and placed more than ten thousand soldiers in the castle. Thus the Moslem troops were driven desperate and obliged to withdraw. Previously to this they had run their ships into the river; and the water having subsided, they were left on the land; and not being able to put them to sea again, they were obliged to fire them.

They then went over-land to Jajl, taking with them the prisoners they had taken from the fortress. The distance was sixty miles. At this place were stationed Oruj's ship and Khair-ad-din's galley of twenty-four benches. Oruj Reis remained at Jajl, whilst Khair-ad-din with three ships proceeded to Tunis, where he bought four others, and with seven volunteer ships, making in all fourteen, he put out to sea. Soon after he was joined by Kurd Oghli Mussaleh-ad-din Reis with fourteen ships; and his fleet now consisting of twenty-eight sail, he proceeded to the infidel coasts. Near Genoa he saw eight barges laden with corn, and having made himself known, they suffered themselves to be taken without any resistance. On his return he met twelve more, all which he also took. These were laden with cloth. The twenty barges he sent by Kurd Oghli to Tunis, whilst he himself went to join his brother.

DEPARTURE OF ORUJ REIS TO ALGIERS.

At this time there was in the harbour opposite the castle of Jezaier (Algiers) a small fortress on an island about an arrow-shot from the city. The Spanish infidels had by some means obtained possession of this castle, and had thus in a manner shut in the inhabitants of the town. The unfortunate Algerines were therefore obliged to submit to them and pay tribute; till at last the oppression of the infidels became insupportable, and they wrote a letter of invitation to Oruj Reis. This letter Oruj received at Jajl, and having perused it, made preparations for his departure. The castle of Jajl he gave in charge to his brother, and came to Algiers. There being here no regular governor, he entered the town and took up his abode in it. Khair-ad-din also sent nearly three hundred men to Jajl, whilst he himself returned to Tunis; and as he was engaged with Kurd Oghli in dividing the plunder, he met his brother Is'hak, who had just arrived at that place with the two ships from the emperor and another from Gallipoli.

ATTACK OF THE FRENCH UPON TUNIS.

The proceedings of Khair-ad-din Reis having surprised and alarmed the infidel nations, the French became enraged, and sent a fleet of thirty-three triremes against Tunis. On their arrival they landed at Benzarta; and Kurd Oghli being there at the time, he left his ships and went into the castle. The infidels having made an assault, took four of the ships; but as they were about to attack the fortress, the troops of Tunis came out against them, fought bravely, and repelled them. The infidels in haste betook themselves to their ships, leaving six in the harbour, and proceeded to Halk-al-vad. Here also Khair-ad-din was in readiness, and valiantly repulsed them, not even suffering them to land; so that they were obliged to return disappointed. About this time Sultan Selim having conquered Egypt, Kurd Oghli went to meet him with magnificent presents; and having paid his respects to him, reported their engagement with the French. Khair-ad-din on the other hand fitted up four ships with five hundred men and cannons, which he sent with his eldest brother to Algiers, whilst he wintered at Tunis.

DEFEAT OF THE INFIDEL FLEET AND THE ARAB TRIBES AT ALGIERS.

When the Arab tribes and the infidels heard that Oruj Reis had obtained possession of Algiers, the latter prepared to attack that place with a fleet of forty galleys and one hundred and forty barges, containing fifteen thousand men. The Arab troops likewise, having marched by land, arrived before the infidels in the neighbourhood of Algiers. Oruj Reis with his followers being prepared for battle, first attacked the Arab troops on the land side, and killed great numbers of them. By the favour of God he was victorious, and the Arabs were routed and obliged to fly, leaving behind them nearly twelve thousand camels. After this the infidel fleet arrived, and having anchored near the castle, they began to land their men and take out their cannon. The castle being in a dilapidated state, Oruj Reis was repairing the breaches when the enemy made a sudden assault, and erected their standard on the fortifications. Oruj Reis now led on his heroes against them, and a hot engagement ensued. By the favour of God they were again crowned with victory, and succeeded in taking the standard of the infidels, whom they pursued and killed whilst flying to their ships. Only one thousand of them escaped, who, entering their ships, set sail and departed. After this Oruj Reis settled in Algiers, and the infidels were constantly harassed and routed. He then sent information of his victory to Khair-ad-din, to whom he offered the charge of the castle, as also that of Jajl. Khair-ad-din accordingly went to Jajl, and securing the sheikh-al-balad, made him engage to pay the annual tribute which he was in the habit of transmitting to the infidels. After this he departed and joined his brother.

THE CAPTURE OF TUNIS.

Previously to the above affair, the beg of Tilmisan's brother had gone to Spain, and returning with assistance, had taken Tunis. The inhabitants of that place having sought redress from Oruj Reis, he sent his brother Khair-ad-din to their assistance.   On the arrival of Khair-ad-din the infidels had left their ships, and taken possession of the castle. He then secured their ships, landed his men, and after a siege of two days, the enemy capitulated, and gave up the castle. Hefs Zadeh also fled, and Khair-ad-din, not being able to find him, enriched himself with plunder, and returned to Algiers.   The two brothers then divided the castles belonging to Algiers and Bajaia.   These were ten in number; five on the east side of Algiers, and five on the west.   Those on the east were assigned to Khair-ad-din Beg, and the others to Oruj Beg; a census being taken of the population of each division.

THE CAPTURE OF TILMISAN.

The governor of Tilmisan was at this time tributary to the king of Spain, and was obliged to transmit his tribute annually. Being alarmed by hearing that Oruj Beg and his brother had become masters of Algiers, he entered into negotiations with Spain to assist him in removing them from that place. But just as the Spanish fleet and his own land forces were preparing for the expedition, Oruj Beg was apprised of it, and leaving his brother at Algiers, went off with a few troops to Tilmisan. The inhabitants of this latter place having united with the infidels, and disobeyed their magistrates, the Ulemas had pronounced fatvas or decrees o death against them; but on the approach of Oruj, the commercial intercourse between the principal men and the other inhabitants was resumed. The governor being detected, was obliged to fly; and his two brothers, who were in confinement, availing themselves of the opportunity, made their escape, and fled to Fez. The governor, however, went to the port of Tilmisan called Vehran (Oran), and craved assistance of the Spaniards, who were then in the possession of that port. They forthwith gave him large supplies both of money and forces; and in addition to these, he collected by land about fifteen thousand Arabs, with whom, and fifteen hundred infidel matchlock men, he left Vehran, and came to Kalat-al-kala.   Khair-ad-din being informed of this, sent his brother Is'hak Reis, with a few troops, to defend it.   As soon as Is'hak had entered the castle the infidel troops arrived, and laid siege to it.   One night Oruj Reis made a sally, in which he killed about seven hundred infidels, and took a hundred prisoners; but shortly after the enemy were reinforced by the arrival of ten thousand infidels and twenty thousand

Arabs, an event which served to protract the siege for six months, during which time several battles were fought with equal fierceness and desperation on both sides. At length the towers fell, and the besieged, now become desperate, rushed out, and commenced plundering the enemy's camp: a massacre ensued, and Is'hak, the brother of Oruj, and his followers fell. Having taken Kalat-al-kala, the infidels proceeded to Tilmisan, which they blockaded. Oruj Reis with his attendants betook himself to the inner citadel, and there remained shut up for seven months; during which period fierce encounters occasionally took place: but at length Oruj with his troops evacuated the citadel, and commenced a general attack upon the infidels. In the engagement which ensued he and his followers suffered martyrdom, and necessity compelled the inhabitants to yield.

ATTACK OF THE INFIDELS UPON ALGIERS.

In the spring the infidels fitted out a fleet of one hundred and seventy ships, which they manned with twenty thousand soldiers, and sailed to Vehran, where they were joined by three or four thousand troops who were stationed in that place. These, under the command of the beg of Tilmisan, proceeded by land to Algiers. Khair-ad-din, on his part, assembled his followers, and having encouraged them, desired the natives to go out to meet the beg of Tilmisan. When they met him they behaved respectfully to him, and abstained from offering any affront to his army. The troops of Khair-ad-din amounted to only six thousand, besides about twenty thousand Arabs whom he had subjugated. When the infidel fleet arrived, they anchored opposite the island, and sent a message demanding the surrender of Algiers. Khair-ad-din Beg thereupon took his station in the field; and when the infidels bore down upon him, they were repulsed with such bravery, that many of them fell; and by the help of God he was completely victorious, and the enemy fled in confusion to their ships. When the evening came on both parties withdrew. The next day they again fought from morning till evening, and on the third day the infidels drew off their field-pieces, and being thrown into the utmost fear and confusion, most of them were routed. Not more than about five or six thousand reached their ships, and escaped. Of the spoil which Khair-ad-din took, he gave a part with a few horses to Hassan, the serasker of Tilmisan, and giving him the command of two thousand Arabs and seven hundred regular troops, sent him back to Tilmisan; but before he could reach it twenty thousand Arabs had risen in arms, and the governor had fled; and when he arrived, of nearly four thousand infidels, about seven hundred had made their escape, and fled to Tunis, the rest having perished in the revolt.

THE CAPTURE OF TUNIS.

In the spring Khair-ad-din Beg being desirous to take this castle, its governor solicited assistance from Spain. Accordingly fifteen barges were sent to defend it ; whilst Khair-ad-din sent eighteen ships, and himself proceeded against it by land. When he arrived at the castle he took it by storm, but with difficulty saved the ships which he had sent, five of which were taken. He then returned to Algiers.

EXECUTION OF THE INFIDEL CHIEFS AT ALGIERS.

About this time, when Khair-ad-din's ships were lying in the harbour, the Admiral Ferdinand from Spain entered it with a fleet of one hundred and ten ships. Khair-ad-din immediately came into the harbour, and after a hot engagement entirely routed the infidels. The admiral's ship struck on the sand, when, in despair, he and six hundred infidels jumped overboard, and, with thirty-six captains, in all about three thousand men, were made prisoners. Two prisons under ground were filled with them, and the city was crowded with those assigned to the natives. Some of them formed a conspiracy, and had made arrangements for their escape, but were detected. Soon after a messenger arrived from Spain offering 100,000 ducats for the ransom of the thirty-six officers. To this the Ulemas would not give their consent ; saying, that the captains being expert in naval matters, and every one of them brave fellows, the sum ought to be doubled : this however was not effected. Khair-ad-din then sought some pretence for having them killed ; and when he heard of their attempt to escape, ordered a general execution. For the body of the Admiral Ferdinand seven thousand florins were offered ; but the Moslems considering it improper to deal in carcases, threw it into a deep well.

THE GOVERNMENT OF KHAIR-AD-DIN BEG AT ALGIERS.

During these transactions Khair-ad-din assembled the citizens of Algiers, and addressed them in these words:—"Hitherto I have given you every assistance, and I have fortified your castle by placing in it four hundred pieces of cannon ; now appoint whom you please as your governor, and I will proceed by sea to some other place." All of them simultaneously began to cry out and beseech him not to leave them. Khair-ad-din answered that the begs of Tunis and Tilmisan were opposed to him ; but that if the khotba* and the coinage were made in the name of the Ottoman Sultan, he would consent to remain with them.   To this they agreed ; and Khair-ad-din having fitted out four vessels, and loaded them with spoils, arms, and various presents, as also forty valiant youths selected from among the prisoners, sent them as a present to Sultan Selim.   The illustrious emperor graciously accepted them, and in return sent him a splendid sabre and a dress of honour, with a sanjak†, which he gave in charge to one Haji Hussein, a servant of the Sublime Court.   But on their way to Algiers eight Venetian galleys attacked them, and killed all the servants of Khair-ad-din Beg. Haji Hussein with three others escaped, and landed at Motone, whence he re-turned to the capital.   On application to the Venetian governor, the ships were restored, and they once more set out for Algiers. On their arrival Khair-ad-din came out to meet them, and received with profound reverence the horse and sanjak, which the emperor had sent him.   He then assembled his divan, and ordered the criers to proclaim the authority of the sultan.   After having given a splendid entertainment to the messenger, and treated him with proper courtesy, he sent him back to the Porte.

INSURRECTION OF THE PEOPLE OF TUNIS AND TILMISAN.

On account of the above proceedings, the begs of Tunis and Tilmisan became jealous, and concerted measures to corrupt Mohammed Beg and Ibn Kazi, two of Khair-ad-din's most powerful begs.   They at last gained them over to their party, and by giving money to the Arabs, would have conquered Algiers; but Khair-ad-din maintained a defensive position, and did not submit to them.

THE CAPTURE OF MUSTAGHANIM.

As was previously mentioned, the two brothers of the beg of Tilmisan had fled to the king of Fez, and he having supplied them with forces, they marched against Tilmisan, and besieged it; but being deserted by their Arabs, Massoud (one of them) came over to Khair-ad-din, whilst his brother fled to Vehran. Khair-ad-din treated Massoud with kindness, and persuaded his Arabs to return

* *Khotba* is an harangue read by the mullahs in the mosques, in which the reigning prince is mentioned and prayed for.

† *Sanjak*, the standard given to governors of districts under begs.

to him : whereupon he again set out against Tilmisan with what forces he could collect, and having put his brother to flight, took the castle. But not long after this he broke his faith with Khair-ad-din, and joined the infidels ; in consequence of which, Khair-ad-din sent assistance to his brother (Abdullah) at Vehran, whence the allies sent an army by land, and twenty-eight ships by sea, to a castle called Mustaghanim, which they reduced. They then sailed to the infidel coasts, which they plundered extensively, and taking on board all the Moslems they could find in Andalusia, returned to Algiers.

THE SECOND CAPTURE OF TILMISAN.

When Abdullah, the brother of Massoud, had left Vehran and come to Tilmisan, with the troops of Khair-ad-din, Massoud came out against him, but was routed in an engagement, and driven into the castle, where he was shut up twenty days. One night, however, two hundred men scaled the castle walls and threw open the outer gates ; but Massoud, who was in the inner castle, made his escape with two hundred horsemen. The criers then proclaimed Sultan Selim sovereign of the place ; and as soon as order was restored Abdullah was duly installed governor by Khair-ad-din. The khotba was read, and coinage was issued in the name of the emperor ; and a garrison of an hundred and fifty men was left in the castle. On the departure of Khair-ad-din, Massoud returned and besieged it for three months ; but the former hastened back to its defence, routed Massoud in an engagement, in which he made him prisoner ; and he died in confinement.

REBELLION OF KAZI-ZADEH.

About this time Kazi-Zadeh, the governor of Tunis, revolted, and having excited the Arab tribes against Khair-ad-din, came and besieged Algiers. The infidels inhabiting a small island near Algiers also effected a passage, and attacked the city on one side. For six months Khair-ad-din was engaged in various battles with the besiegers, but still remained unconquered. At length, on the approach of winter, Kazi-Zadeh was under the necessity of begging a truce, and returned to Tunis. Shortly afterwards, however, he again sent an army against Algiers, under the command of his brother ; but Khair-ad-din came out, and having completely routed them, sent in pursuit of the fugitives Kara

Hassan, one of his attendants, who reduced all the fortresses belonging to Tunis. But Kazi-Zadeh corrupted him also, and induced him to come over to his own party. Khair-ad-din had now nothing left him but the city of Algiers; and even here the inhabitants began to be disaffected. Having discovered that it was the intention of the Arab sheikhs to leave the city, he assembled his followers, who, as about two hundred of the sheikhs were rushing towards the palace, the gate of which opened into three roads, attacked and dispersed them, taking several, whom they put in prison. The followers of Khair-ad-din recommended a general massacre in the city; but this he prevented. In the morning he assembled the citizens at the mosque, and reasoned with them. One hundred and fifty of the insurgents he sent to prison, and dismissed the others; whilst the twenty-five persons who had been the original conspirators met the fate they deserved. Peace was thus restored, which continued for two years.

DEPARTURE OF KHAIR-AD-DIN BEG TO JIJELI.

A misunderstanding afterwards arose between the inhabitants of Algiers and Khair-ad-din Beg, whose troops quarrelled with the natives; and the intercourse between Algiers and the neighbouring places was interrupted. In this state of affairs, Khair-ad-din, being little better than a prisoner, determined on leaving the place; but was undecided as to taking his property with him. While he was perplexed about this matter, and was praying for direction, the Prophet (upon whom be the blessing of God!) appeared to him in a dream, and seemed to him to be commencing in person the operation of placing the warrior's effects in a ship. At this time information had been received of the apprehension of Kara Hassan, with offers to deliver him up. Khair-ad-din, therefore, under the pretence of going to secure him, emptied his house, and in the morning loaded nine vessels with his property, and put on board his family and servants. He then called for the principal men of the town, and the men of Ibn Kazi, who wished to make peace with him, and throwing them the keys of the city, exclaimed, "The troubles of Islamism be upon your shoulders, ye wretches!" mounted his horse, and went down to his ship. That night he lay in the harbour, whilst the Algerines raised a great lamentation, and great and small came to bid him farewell, and entreated him for advice. Khair-ad-din recommended them to God, and telling them to wait three years, and that they might then go where they pleased, he weighed anchor, and sailed for Jijeli.

OPERATIONS OF KHAIR-AD-DIN AT JIJELI.

On his arrival at the castle of Jijeli, which is situated on the coast of Moghreb, and in which he fixed his residence, a great scarcity of provisions arose; to remedy which inconvenience, he went out to sea with seven ships. On the infidels' coast he came up with nine barges laden with provisions, one of which he sunk, and took the remaining eight. With these he returned and produced plenty, for which the people gave thanks. Seven hundred infidels were taken out of these barges. He then built for himself a galley of twenty-seven benches, with which and nine other vessels he began to plunder on the coasts of Tunis, taking prisoners all who had been opposed to him, and burning their ships. Shortly afterwards he met six barges laden with corn in the Gulf of Genoa. When the people on board saw Khair-ad-din, they immediately surrendered their vessels, which he took, and went to Jarba. He now began to recover the favour of the people, and Aidin Reis, Shaaban Reis, and twelve other reises, having heard of his invitation, joined him with forty ships, and sailed on an expedition to the coasts of the infidels, all the towns along which they attacked and plundered ; and having taken many prisoners, and acquired considerable wealth, returned, and most of them wintered at Jijeli.

THE DEFEAT OF KAZI-ZADEH.

As the power of Khair-ad-din now began to increase, Ibn Kazi, from fear of him, sent him presents; but as he was not very peaceably disposed, Khair-ad-din evinced no friendship towards him. About this time some of the ships of the former arrived from Spain with Moslems ; but when they touched at Algiers Kazi-Zadeh would not permit them to land; in consequence of which they came to Jijeli, and laid their complaints before Khair-ad-din. Khair-ad-din, who had been directed in a dream to return to Algiers, rose up and addressed a letter to the sheikhs of that place, inviting them to join him. This invitation they accepted, and came over to him. Kazi-Zadeh, being informed of this, collected an army of twenty thousand men, and came out to meet Khair-ad-din, prepared to give him battle. He was defended on one side by a mountain, at the foot of which he raised a mound ; but when the two armies engaged, he was put to the rout, and four thousand of his Arabs were killed. He then took refuge in a fastness of the mountain ; but Khair-ad-din coming upon him, killed him, and put to flight part of his army. The number of his matchlock men did not exceed eighteen hundred. After this event, the Arab sheikhs from all quarters came and joined Khair-ad-din, who, by proper management recovered all his former possessions. When these transactions reached the ear of Kara Hassan, he fled with five hundred men to Sharshal; but Khair-ad-din pursued him with speed, attacked the rebel, took him prisoner, and put him to death.

RETURN OF KHAIR-AD-DIN BEG TO ALGIERS.

Khair-ad-din when he left Algiers promised to return in three years ; and that period having now expired, he fulfilled his promise, and once more entered that city. This hero was in the habit of seeking Divine guidance in all his affairs, and foresaw in visions most of the circumstances attending the battles he fought. The Arabs now attached themselves to him, and the people enjoyed security and ease. Abdullah, the beg of Tilmisan, having for six years refused to transmit his annual tribute of ten thousand ducats, and having joined himself with the infidels, and issued the khotba and the coinage in his own name, Khair-ad-din sent him an admonitory epistle ; to which however he paid no attention, and preparations for hostilities were commenced on both sides.

THE ENGAGEMENT WITH ABDULLAH.

Abdullah drew out his Arab troops, whilst Khair-ad-din marched against him from Algiers, and his efforts being crowned with success, he routed Abdullah, who fled, leaving behind him only eight thousand camels, which fell into the hands of the victorious troops. Abdullah then sent a messenger to sue for peace; and having read the khotba and issued the coinage in the name of the sultan, a peace was concluded, on condition that he should pay an indemnity of twenty thousand ducats, and an annual sum of ten thousand ducats for six years. His brother Ibn Kazi having also rebelled, Khair-ad-din marched against him, and compelled him to pay thirty *yūks** of silver. Having now overcome most of the difficulties with which he had been surrounded, Khair-ad-din began to think of reducing the island opposite Algiers. On this island, which is about a bow-shot from the city, there was formerly a small fortress, of which the infidels by some means or other had obtained possession ; and when Khair-ad-din took Algiers they filled it with ammunition, and strongly fortified it Previously to that event these infidels exacted a tribute from the citizens ; and whilst the

---

* A *yūk* is one hundred thousand aspres, or a thousand dollars.

Moslems were calling to prayers from the minarets, were accustomed to discharge the artillery, and thus did considerable injury. On the arrival of Khair-ad-din Beg at Algiers, they petitioned him to allow them to remain unmolested in their fortress, promising at the same time never to set foot within the city. Khair-ad-din however would not consent to a peace, but continued to annoy them. This state of things had now continued fourteen years, when Khair-ad-din Beg blockaded the castle; and hearing that the king of Spain had resolved to send to its succour, he continued his attacks night and day for a whole week. The besieged then begged for quarter; but this he refused, and took the castle sword in hand. Besides those who were killed, about five hundred men were taken prisoners. He then ordered that the castle should be rased, and the passage filled up, so that the centre might form a harbour; and it accordingly forms the present harbour of Algiers. He next made the infidels repair those parts of the town which they had destroyed with their cannon, and put their chiefs to death. Nine barges which had come to their assistance from Spain, not being able to find the castle, were about to return, when Khair-ad-din pursued them with fifteen galleys; took them all by force of arms, and returned to Algiers. Besides those who fell in the engagement, one thousand seven hundred men were made prisoners.

The moral this event teaches is, that a barge may be taken by a galley provided the commander of the latter be an experienced person.

THE WARS OF AIDIN REIS.

The admiral who had been taken in the above-mentioned expedition having informed them that the king of Spain had gone to Genoa, Khair-ad-din Beg appointed Aidin Reis to the command of his fleet, and sent him towards that quarter. The reis, sailing towards the infidel territories, plundered the coast about Marseilles, and took many Mudagils.* Fifteen vessels that had been sent from Spain to protect these parts were now cruising about; and Aidin Reis being desirous of attacking them, commenced a vigorous pursuit, and at length came up with them whilst they were lying off a barren island. A fierce engagement

---

* مدجل This name is frequently given throughout the work to the Andalusian Moors; but I have never seen it used by any other author, nor can I discover its origin. The only instance in which a similar word occurs is in the following passage in Don Quixote: "The Moors of Arragon are in Barbary called Tagarins; and those of Grenada go by the name of *Mudajares*." — Story of the Captive.

F

ensued, in which Aidin Reis took the admiral's ship, and the others were volun-
tarily surrendered.   Three of these ships he emptied and sunk, three he burned,
and the rest he brought to Algiers.   Khair-ad-din then reported this victory to
the Porte.

APPEARANCE OF ANDREA DORIA, AND ATTACK OF KHAIR-AD-DIN.

When the infidel nations could no longer navigate the seas, and there was no
safety along their coasts, the king of Spain called a council to determine what
measures were to be adopted against Barbarossa.*   (Barbarossa in Italian signifies one with a red beard.)   Andrea Doria, one of the most valiant admirals of
Spain, taking his hat in his hand, said, if the king of France would give him
twenty of his galleys he would venture to attack Barbarossa.   Spain had at
this time concluded peace with France, and accordingly sent thither an ambassador to request the galleys.   France, in order to preserve the peace, complied, and
the galleys, together with the Spanish fleet, were given to Andrea, who with a
complete army on board, sailed for Algiers.   Khair-ad-din, on the other hand,
equipped thirty-five ships at Algiers, and invited Senan Reis from Jarba, who
fitted out seven vessels, and joined him.   Khair-ad-din Beg had hoped to meet
Andrea at Majorca; and in anticipation of this had fortified the castle of Sharshal,
which he filled with Mudagils.   But Andrea suddenly changed his course, and
early one morning came upon Sharshal with forty ships, and landed his men.   As
they were about to commence their work of destruction, the Moslems came out of
the castle, and after a fierce engagement, put the infidels to flight.   Before they
could reach their ships four hundred fell by the sword, and six hundred and
forty were made prisoners.   The rest got on board, and made their escape.
When Khair-ad-din arrived he put all the captives in chains.   Among these
was Andrea's steward, from whom they ascertained that his master was
bound for Genoa, there to obtain a reinforcement of troops.   Khair-ad-din therefore immediately sailed for that quarter; and having ascertained in the vicinity
of Marseilles that Andrea had on his way passed near to that place, he went to
an island about thirty miles from thence, and lay off there ten days.   Here they
took a vessel that was passing by laden with cheeses from Majorca, which had
previously been taken near Toulon, a celebrated French port not far from Marseilles; but through the negligence of the warriors on board the goletta stationed
there as a guard-ship by Khair-ad-din, the captain made his escape with his own

* The name by which Khair-ad-din is generally called in European histories.

ship and four others, and gave information respecting Khair-ad-din.   The captain then returned to the fortress, whilst Khair-ad-din turned towards the Genoese coasts, and early next morning attacked a castle on the coast, which he succeeded in capturing, and took the inhabitants prisoners.   In the harbour he found twenty-two ships; all of which he burnt, and demolished the castle.   He then directed his course towards Genoa; but was driven back by a storm to the island off which he had formerly been lying; and here he remained until the storm had subsided.

THE FLIGHT OF ANDREA.

Andrea not being able to reach Genoa from Sharshal, entered a large river in Spain, and thence demanded from Genoa three thousand men, and a supply of gunpowder and arms.   These the Genoese had already forwarded in two large ships to the place where he was lying.   The storm however drove them to Khair-ad-din's place of rendezvous, and one morning one of them passed near his fleet, which, immediately the sail appeared, weighed anchor, and ten vessels proceeded to attack her; when, after a fierce combat, she was taken and brought into port. A few hours afterwards the other ship also made her appearance; but owing to the approach of evening was too late to enter the·harbour, and remained out at sea. That night therefore they did not molest her; but the next morning, as she was preparing to enter the harbour, Khair-ad-din gave orders to commence an attack upon her from a distance. Senan Reis however disobeyed these orders, and going too near, had a musket-ball aimed at him, and was obliged to return into the harbour; but Khair-ad-din, keeping up a distant fire upon the ship, gradually weakened her; and the infidels on board perceiving she began to leak, threw themselves into the sea, and were immediately made prisoners. The warriors then towed the ship to the shore, where they plundered her, and then sunk the hulk.   They then dressed their wounded and buried their dead; first reading over them the prayers appropriated for the funerals of martyrs.   This being done, they put all the infidels in chains, and set fire to the ship which they had first taken.   Khair-ad-din having obtained from those on board these vessels information respecting Andrea, returned to the Arab shores.   Andrea then left the river, and passing through the Strait of Gibraltar, went and lay in the harbour of Seville; whilst Khair-ad-din on his part returned to Algiers.

Some time previous to this the Sultan Soleiman Khan had sent out Mustaffa, one of the *chiaoush** of the Sublime Court, to obtain information respecting a

* *Chiaoush*, a messenger of the Porte.

peace that had been concluded with the king of France, and several other affairs. Khair-ad-din therefore wrote down all the particulars he had been able to obtain, and transmitted them by Mustaffa to the Porte. About this time also the son of Khair-ad-din, Hassan Beg, (who by his mother's side was descended from the Prophet,) with some other reises, made two expeditions to Teiomlek, and took immense booty.

ATTACK OF ANDREA DORIA UPON CORONE, AND REBELLION OF THE GOVERNOR OF TILMISAN.

The Sultan Soleiman Khan having in the year 938 (A. D. 1531-2) gone on an expedition into Germany, Charles V., king of Spain, came to Genoa, and suggested to the Genoese government that as the Grand Toork (i. e. the Great Turk) was engaged in war, a favourable opportunity offered to plunder the Roumelian coasts : but his brother Ferdinand, emperor of Germany, despatched a letter to him, intimating that there would be no great merit in attacking two or three castles, and requesting that he would rather come to his assistance by land. With this request he complied ; and at the same time resolved to send his fleet, under the command of Andrea, to Motone. In order also to divert the attention of Barbarossa, he sent men to excite the beg of Tilmisan to revolt ; and for this purpose he sent fourteen vessels to aid him in an expedition against Algiers. Khair-ad-din was at this time preparing for a voyage to the Sublime Porte ; but immediately left his fleet at sea, and marched to meet the enemy by land. The two armies met in a desert, where a battle took place, and Abdullah, the beg of Tilmisan, was routed, and fled back to Tilmisan. At the intercession of certain persons, peace was restored, on the beg's paying thirty thousand pieces of gold ; and Khair-ad-din returned to Algiers. Andrea now, finding the sea clear, sailed towards the coast of the Morea, and attacked and took the fortress of Corone ; the Capudan Ahmed Pasha, who had this year gone to sea with eighty vessels, arriving too late to save it.

In the Moghreb districts, Khair-ad-din having reduced the land side, sent his chiefs with fifteen vessels to the Spanish coast, where they burnt and destroyed the towns. Fifteen ships which had formerly been taken by the Spaniards were now found at an island called Kïounlugé, where an engagement took place, in which the Spaniards saved only one of them, and the remaining fourteen were brought to Algiers, where the immense booty they contained was divided.

STATE OF THE MUDAGILS OF SPAIN.

Charles V. having gone by land to the assistance of Germany, was obliged to return disappointed and mortified. Before his time the Moslems who remained in the Andalusian towns, though they paid taxes, were allowed to call publicly to prayers, and to exercise their religious ceremonies. But when Charles became king, he issued a proclamation forbidding any one to worship according to the forms of Islamism, and commenced the work of immolation among the faithful. The Moslems, being able to endure this no longer, began to form themselves into societies, and at length convened a general meeting, and took up their position behind a mountain, whence they sent to beg assistance from Khair-ad-din, who immediately sent over thirty-six golettas. On their arrival they bravely withstood the troops that came out to prevent the embarkation of the Moslems. A thousand men were stationed on the field, whilst seven voyages were performed; and all the Moslems were thus conveyed to the opposite shore, and delivered from the power of the infidels. On their passage they captured several vessels, and enriched themselves with plunder. On this occasion about seventy thousand Mudagils were brought over, who settled in Algiers and other places. This is the reason why most of the Algerines are Andalusians.

THE STRATAGEMS OF ANDREA AND OF KHAIR-AD-DIN.

When Sultan Soleiman Khan returned from his expedition into Germany, he sent a letter by Senan Chiaoush to Khair-ad-din Beg, saying that he intended to undertake an expedition against Spain ; and requesting him to appoint some trusty person to govern Algiers in his stead, and proceed forthwith to the Sublime Porte; and that if he could find no such person, he would inform his highness. When it became known that Khair-ad-din was about to set out for the Porte, Andrea left Seville, and came to Genoa ; and in order to prevent him from going, had recourse to the stratagem of sending to Algiers a barge laden with a quantity of merchandise, worth six thousand pieces of gold, and seventy of the prisoners he had taken at Corone, with instructions to inform Khair-ad-din that the king of Spain intended to come against Algiers. Khair-ad-din perceiving the trick, made a feint of unmanning his fleet, and casting trenches ; and having emptied the barge of its cargo, allowed the men to depart; who, on their arrival at Genoa, gave out that Barbarossa had abandoned his intention of going to the Porte. This intelligence pleased Andrea, who immediately proceeded towards Corone.

EXECUTION OF THE INFIDEL CHIEFS.

Among the infidel chiefs who were taken in the two ships before mentioned*
there were twenty men of rank, and captains, and one hundred and twenty brave
infidels, who wore golden chains about their necks. One of the captains was the
son of the grand-master, ($\mu\varepsilon\gamma\alpha$ $\mu\alpha\gamma\iota\sigma\tau\omega\rho$,) who had been sent out from Rhodes;
and when the agents of the Genoese government arrived to treat for their ransom,
they offered large sums (amounting in the whole to 20,000 pieces of gold) for him
and several of the captains. This offer the begs were disposed to accept; but the
ulema (priests) prevented them, saying, "That as these were powerful enemies,
it would be imprudent to give them their liberty." The unfortunate prisoners
were thus left to despair. To keep them prisoners at Algiers was deemed im-
politic; and to put them to death seemed scarcely more advisable; for, in either
case, it was certain that the infidels would employ the money intended for their
ransom in purchasing Moslem captives for the purpose of putting out their eyes,
since they had previously to this cut off the noses and ears of several Moslem
chiefs, cutting the cartilages, and otherwise maiming them; upon which Khair-
ad-din had sent a remonstrance to them, which had the effect of making them
desist from torturing their captives. Thus it was that Saleh Reis and Torghudjeh, who were captives, escaped the torture. Khair-ad-din however anticipated
the consequences of retaining his prisoners; for having seen in a dream that the
captains had murdered the jailer, with a view to effect their escape, he, by
way of experiment, instructed the latter, who was one of his relations, to in-
gratiate himself with the prisoners, and endeavour to discover their secret. This
he effected; and so entirely did he possess their confidence, that they intrusted
him with a letter to the governor of Bajaiah, requesting him to send them a ship,
and informing him that it was their intention to murder the guard of the prison,
and thus make their escape; that there were seven thousand prisoners in
Algiers; and that if they did not succeed in taking the city, they should at all
events escape from prison. Having first showed this letter to Khair-ad-din, the
jailer proceeded to Bajaiah to deliver it. On his arrival there he delivered the
letter; and a vessel was immediately prepared and sent off, so as to reach the
prisoners that night. The jailer, having been treated with the greatest respect,
returned, and related all that had passed to Khair-ad-din, who immediately sent
out a vessel to seize the one sent from Bajaiah, which had just arrived; when
the infidels on board, about 120 in number, together with the captains in the
prison, were put to death, on the above accusation. Their letters he sent to the
Genoese, who recognised the handwriting, and necessarily kept silence.

* See p. 43.

DEPARTURE OF KHAIR-AD-DIN FOR THE CAPITAL.

Khair-ad-din having thus disposed of most of the captives, appointed Hassan Beg, one of his most faithful servants, governor in his stead, and with several vessels fully equipped sailed for the Sublime Porte, in order to pay his respects.* Passing by Sardinia and Sicily, he went on to Genoa, near which place he one morning suddenly attacked and plundered a castle.　Before this was made generally known he left Genoa, and proceeded towards Messina.　On his passage thither he met eighteen barges, all of which he took, and made the infidels on board prisoners; and on approaching the town set fire to the barges.　Being informed that Andrea with twenty-four galleys and twenty-six barges had gone to Corone, he sailed to Prevesa, whence the infidels sent intelligence to Andrea that Barbarossa was seeking him, and cautioned him to be on his guard : and in consequence of this information he went and secured himself in Brindisi.　Khair-ad-din, hearing this, sent twenty-five vessels in pursuit of him.　These overtook seven Anapolitan ships that were following Andrea, five of which made their escape to Anapoli; and the other two they took, and returned to Khair-ad-din.　At this time Khair-ad-din and his fleet had arrived at Navarin, where he had an interview with the Capudan Ahmed Beg.　He then proceeded to Corone, and there liberated a few of his captives.　On his arrival at the Straits he received a pressing invitation from the emperor (whose glory is like that of Jemshid) to enter Constantinople, which he did, amid the firing of numerous salutes.

ARRIVAL OF KHAIR-AD-DIN AT THE SUBLIME PORTE.

On that day, which was about the middle of the year 940 (A. D. 1533), the vessels were moored opposite Galata ; and on the morning following Khair-ad-din entered the house of the Capudan Ahmed Beg, in the At Meidan, which had been appointed for his reception.　On the divan day, he went to the divan, taking with him eighteen reises his companions, and rich presents, where he had the honour of kissing the royal hand, and had innumerable favours conferred upon him.　The reises were also admitted into the august presence ; and having kissed the royal hand, each received a dress of honour and had a stipend allotted him ; and his majesty commanded that they should be sent to the royal arsenal, and there exercise their skill in constructing vessels.

* Literally, *to rub his face on the threshold.*

KHAIR-AD-DIN GOES TO ALEPPO.

The illustrious emperor being prepared to set out on his sixth expedition'
(which was to be to the Irakin,*) in the above-mentioned year (940), in the
month Rabi-al-Akher, (Oct. or Nov. 1533,) sent forward the Grand Vezier Ibrahim Pasha to winter at Aleppo. This general now sent a letter of invitation to
Khair-ad-din, with a request that the emperor would allow him to depart. The emperor having at this time directed all his forces, both military and naval, to that
quarter, expressed in an interview with Khair-ad-din his consent to his departure. Khair-ad-din then set out by land; and on his arrival at Aleppo, the
vezier called a divan, and performing the ceremonies of the istakbal,† showed
him great respect. Khair-ad-din, having according to custom kissed hands, had
a place assigned him under all the begs and pashas. Next day, however,
when he came to the assembly, he was clothed, according to the custom of the
Osmanlis, with the robe of the begler-beg of Algiers, and took his seat above
all the other begler-begs. After two or three days spent in feasting and trans-
acting unimportant business, he was sent back to the Porte, where he arrived in
twenty-four days, and resumed his affairs.

* *Irakin*, the name given to two countries, one of which, generally called Irak Arabi, is Babylo-
nia; and the other, Irak Adgemi, or Persian Irak, is a large province of Persia.

† *Istakbal*, a ceremonious procession to meet any great man.

CHAPTER III.

Respecting the affairs of Khair-ad-din, from the time of his being made Capudan of the fleet.

THE pasha, on his return from Aleppo, built sixty-one *bashderdes** and galleys, with which and eighteen vessels which he brought with him from Algiers and five private ones, in all eighty-four, he was ordered out to sea.

THE FIRST EXPEDITION OF KHAIR-AD-DIN PASHA.

On a propitious day Khair-ad-din Pasha sailed with the above-mentioned eighty-four vessels, and went towards Messina, where he demolished the castle of Reggio, which had been evacuated by the infidels. That night he lay with lantern lights, and prayed for success in an expedition he contemplated against Malta. Having had a favourable dream, he arose and set sail during the night, and by morning reached a castle called Santalohso, which he took and plundered. Seven thousand eight hundred prisoners were taken, and the fortress rased. In the evening he again sailed, and reached a fortress called Giatros, where he landed his men, took it by the sword, and made the people prisoners. Here he found eighteen full-built vessels, which, with the castle and houses, he entirely destroyed. After this he went again to sea, and took another castle in the neighbourhood of Anapoli, the people of which he also took captive. Passing thence, he sailed a day and a night, and attacked the castle of Sperlonca, where he took ten thousand prisoners, and levelled the fortress with the ground. He then proceeded onwards, attacked the island of Sardinia, and having plundered

---

* *Bashderdé*, a commander's galley.

G

it, turned his course towards Algiers; but the weather driving him to the Arab shores, he was about to proceed to the castle of Bekerzet, when the governor abandoned it, and went to acquaint Hefs, the king of Tunis.

KHAIR-AD-DIN'S EXPEDITION AGAINST TUNIS, AND THE ATTACK OF THE INFIDELS UPON THAT CITY.

At this period the kingdom of Tunis was held by the Beni Hefs, Sultan Hassan, the twentieth king of that branch, being the reigning monarch. His brother Rashid had some time before this gone with Khair-ad-din to the Porte, where a provision had been made for him.* Khair-ad-din was exceedingly anxious to add to the possessions of the Sublime Power the city of Tunis, and particularly the castle of Halk-al-vad (Goletta), on account of the conveniences it afforded for the wintering of a fleet, and its being a well secured place; and on representing to his majesty the expediency of his project, he was charged with the reduction of the place.

The Tunisians at this time were discontented with Sultan Hassan, and Khair-ad-din coming against them ostensibly in the company of Rashid, who however remained at Constantinople, was directed to Halk-al-vad. Hassan now took to flight, whereupon Khair-ad-din left the castle of Halk-al-vad, and entered the city of Tunis, which was nine miles distant. The partisans of the Hefsi now held out the hand of submission to Khair-ad-din, who collected and imprisoned them in the castle, executing a few of the sheikhs. Hassan then commenced an attack from the outside, and Khair-ad-din going without the gates, a fierce battle ensued. Three hundred Arabs fell, and Hassan was routed and fled. Khair-ad-din having thus subdued Tunis, wrote letters to all the Arab Meshaiekh, and adopted measures for the apprehension of Hassan. He also brought a few troops from Algiers, and registered the subjects. The Tunisians having at length discovered that Rashid was not with Khair-ad-din, became discontented and rebellious: but order was speedily restored by putting to death some of the insurgents. Hassan, on the other hand, collected a force at Kairavan, (Cyrene,) whilst

---

* Rashid had been supplanted by his brother Hassan, and applied to Khair-ad-din for assistance in regaining his kingdom. Khair-ad-din, eager to add Tunis to his other possessions, induced Rashid to accompany him to Constantinople, under the pretence of obtaining the aid of the Ottoman arms. On their arrival there, Khair-ad-din communicated his designs to the sultan, who immediately gave orders for the preparation of a fleet. Rashid already considered himself restored to his kingdom; but just as the fleet was about to sail, he was seized by the command of the sultan, and was never after heard of. Such was the *provision* made for him at the Sublime Porte!

Khair-ad-din with his Arab troops, consisting of ten thousand men, and thirty cannons, the carriages of which were propelled by sails, marched from Tunis into the desert.   The battle was commenced by the firing of the artillery, and the enemy, unable to maintain their ground against cannon and musketry, fled in confusion.   Hassan being thus again routed, the Arab sheikhs came over and submitted themselves to Khair-ad-din.   At this time a brother of Hassan, Abdul-momin, considering the absence of the Sultan Soleiman Khan in Persia afforded a favourable opportunity for his enterprise, went over to Tripoli.   Charles, king of Spain, also, excited by the Pope, united with Portugal, embarked twenty-four thousand troops on board three hundred barges and galleys, and made preparations for sailing.   Just at this time Hassan sent a message to the latter, informing them that he had besieged Barbarossa with his Arab army in Tunis, and inviting them to come and take him prisoner.   They thereupon immediately resolved to go and take Tunis, and then to resume their intended course.   On the seventh day they arrived, and entered the harbour by the left tower, near the castle of Halk-al-vad, where they landed their men.   When the Tunisians saw the infidels they joined Khair-ad-din ; and the castle of Halk-al-vad being rather confined, the besieged cast a trench about it, raised tabors,* and disposed their artillery.   The infidel forces having fixed their camps, for several days fierce engagements were fought, and more than six thousand of the enemy were slain; but as they constantly received fresh assistance from their rear, they kept their ground, and continued the assault : they also raised mounds, and strengthened themselves with one hundred and twenty pieces of cannon, which they landed from their ships.   For thirty-two days and nights they kept up an incessant attack upon the castle, which exhausted their stock of ammunition.   Thrice did the Moslems force their mound, on each occasion killing great numbers of the infidels; but the attack of the latter was so violent, that, finding it impossible to hold out any longer, they were obliged to evacuate the castle and secure themselves in Tunis.----The infidels then took possession of it, when Sultan Hassan, coming up with a few Arabs, mixed his own troops with the infidels, and sent letters, holding forth great promises, to his friends in Tunis.   The Tunisians were at this time divided into four parties ; one of them consisting of the people of the castle, and the other three of Mar'esh.   Khair-ad-din having assembled these parties, thus addressed them : " You have received letters from the infidels : what is *your* intention ?   *I* shall go out and fight, but *you* may remain in the city."   They cried out, " God forbid !" and swore they would accompany him.   Nine thousand seven hundred men ac-

* *Tabor*, a Polish word, signifying a wall or fence made with the baggage, carriages, &c.

cordingly went out with him, the party that had seemed favourable to the enemy joining them, though against their inclination. When the infidels approached the castle, Khair-ad-din attacked them, and fought bravely. A few Algerines having made their appearance in the rear, the infidels turned back, and the Algerines pursued and killed many of them. The enemy being now on the point of making a retreat, the party that had been standing neuter fled towards the castle, Khair-ad-din sent men to induce them to return; but failing in his object, the others too began to fly, and he then removed his artillery to the castle. The infidels supposing that the Turks had fled, began to return, but after some slight skirmishing, as the evening drew on they retired to their tents. Next morning Khair-ad-din having raised a mound about the fortress, and sent his Algerines forward, leaving a person called Giafer Agha in charge of the city, shortly afterwards followed them himself. The infidels, being now greatly distressed by reason of the great heat and the scarcity of water, were about to retreat, when the Tunisians evacuated the city and fled. There were only four thousand captives, who immediately freed themselves and shut the gates. According to one account, the above-mentioned Giafer Beg had joined the opposite party of Tunis, and had persuaded them to leave the place. The infidels having taken to flight, when it was over Khair-ad-din, with about two hundred men who had stood by him, pursued the fugitive Tunisians, and turning them from the direction which Hassan's army had taken, brought them into the road leading to Bajaiah. The infidels in the mean time came back, took possession of the city, and placed Hassan on the throne. At his request they repaired the fortress of Halk-al-vad, and garrisoned it with four thousand soldiers. The vile race who had been the cause of the insurrection, and who remained in the castle, were accused of adherence to Rashid, and the greater part of them publicly executed.

KHAIR-AD-DIN'S RETURN TO ALGIERS.

About this time Khair-ad-din had given the fortress of Beled-al-enab in charge to a certain capudan, whom he sent thither with fifteen small vessels. On his arrival there, hearing of the attack of the infidels upon Tunis, he sunk the vessels by order of the pasha. On the fifth day after the above events Khair-ad-din went to Bajaiah, and thence to Beled-al-enab, where he gave orders that each reis should bring out his vessel, and placing several pieces of cannon at the mouth of the river, he repulsed the infidel ships that attempted to approach. Having fully equipped the vessels, he sailed for Algiers, the inhabitants of which came out to meet him. After having had an interview with his family, the pasha began to equip the nine vessels which were lying there under the command of Murad Agha, with which and eight private Algerine ones, after a stay of fifteen days, he went out to sea, having in all thirty-two vessels under his command. He first anchored at a place about thirty miles from Majorca, and early the next morning a salute of fifty-six guns was fired from the castle. The pasha, telling his people they should learn the cause of all this afterwards, then made sail, and on his way took two barges, in which were some Tunisian captives. These he set free; but put the infidels into chains, and burnt their ships. From Minorca he sailed to a castle called Milota, into the harbour of which he entered with infidel colours. The infidel fleet had put into this port on its way to Tunis, and now when Khair-ad-din approached the castle, the infidels, supposing it to be Andrea's fleet on its return, fired a salute. Two Portuguese barges that were coming in with a fair wind, when they saw Khair-ad-din's fleet tacked and were about to fly, but on hearing the salute returned and anchored. Several infidels then came from the castle to learn the news about Tunis; these Khair-ad-din seized and put into chains. He also sent two boats to the barges with the intimation, "Come along—Barbarossa wants you:" a mandate which the terrified infidels obeyed; and ninety prisoners found on board were liberated.

When Khair-ad-din came to these islands,* a report had been spread that his intention was to plunder them, and the inhabitants were in consequence greatly alarmed. The governor, in order to comfort them, sent them a prisoner dressed like the pasha, with a message that the king, having taken Barbarossa, had sent him to them that they might burn him. The captive was accordingly burnt, and this gave occasion to the salute. When however the capture of Minorca was made known, the circumstance afforded a source of ridicule to the captives.

CAPTURE OF THE CASTLE OF MINORCA†.

Khair-ad-din having landed his men, laid siege to this castle; and when the attack had lasted four days, the governor of the island came out with six thousand infidels, when, after a furious engagement, he was routed, and his horse being

---

* *These islands.* In the text the word is جزاير by which also Algiers is called; but it being also the form of the Arabic plural of جزيره‎ *an island,* and the Turkish plural, جزيرلر‎ occurring a little after, I am inclined to think that the islands of Majorca, Minorca, &c are meant.

† In the original it is Majorca, but from the context this appears to be a mistake, which indeed might easily be made, the difference between منورقة and ميورقة‎ being small. Hammer in his " *Geschichte des Osmanischen Reichs*," in a note on this event makes it Minorca.

hamstrung, he fell, and was killed on the spot. The infidels, seeing this, surrendered the castle. Khair-ad-din then abandoned the wealth of the place to the
plunder of his warriors. Five thousand seven hundred prisoners were taken, and
eight hundred were killed: and on the sixth day Khair-ad-din rased the fortress
and returned to Algiers.

CAUSE OF THE COWARDICE OF THE INFIDELS.

At the last-mentioned siege the Moslems had to resist the infidel begs for some
days, on account of their superior numbers: for had they not possessed this
advantage, they would not have fought in the position which Khair-ad-din
had taken; since it is written in their books that it is lawful to fall alive
into the enemy's hand, and that they who fall in battle do not enter
paradise; their learned men also teach this doctrine. It is related that
Andrea Doria once asked a learned captive the reason why our race were
so brave in battle. The captive replied that it was a miracle performed
by our prophet, because that whoever received his faith became brave, and
would draw his sword even against his own relatives. Andrea asked a
farther reason, but the captive could not give him any other, and said he knew
no more on the subject. Andrea then said, " Is it not written in your books
that whoever flies from battle goes to hell, and that if a person flies from two
infidels he cannot enter paradise? These are the words that make the Moslems
so brave. Now in our books it is written, that if a thousand men should be
attacked by one Moslem, and they know they are to be killed by him, they need
not fight him, because those who die in battle do not enter paradise. This it is
that makes us so cowardly." This doctrine is also taught by the Pope; the
infidel soldiers however fight till they die, caring little about a future state.
The author has questioned several learned men among the Christians on this
subject, and has ascertained that the case is not as stated by Andrea, who
being an ignorant fellow and unacquainted with books, spoke only his own
ideas of the matter. The Christians do not consider it lawful to turn from
battle.

RETURN OF KHAIR-AD-DIN TO THE PORTE.

Whilst the king of Spain was on a visit to the Pope, and was boasting that
he had killed Barbarossa and taken Tunis, the account of the capture of Minorca

reached him, disclosed his falsehood, and obliged him to return with shame to his own country. Andrea having also heard of the fate of Minorca, resolved on going against Barbarossa. The latter had just left Algiers, and on his way came in sight of Andrea's fleet, but not being observed himself, he took no notice of the fleet. The pasha next touched at Jarba, and thence continued his course to the Porte. The emperor at that time had just returned from Bagdad, and Khair-ad-din having paid his respects,* was ordered to build two hundred vessels for an expedition against Puglia, to the completion of which he accordingly applied himself.

THE EXPEDITION TO PUGLIA.

The warlike pasha in the month Rabia-al-akher 943 (Sept. 1536) left the royal arsenal with thirty light vessels, and sailing into the Mediterranean, directed his course to a strong fortress called Castel, which he captured after a hot engagement. Having secured the prisoners, he plundered the fortress, and the winter season having set in, returned to the Porte to repair and refit his fleet.

SULTAN SOLEIMAN'S EXPEDITION TO CORFU.

The cause of this expedition was this. In the time of Sultan Mohammed Khan, the conqueror, the kingdom of Puglia had been subdued, but when Keduk Ahmed Pasha succeeded to it, Spain demanded its restoration. The warlike emperor therefore determined to send a large fleet to that quarter; for the Grand Vizier Eias Pasha represented that the sanjaks of Avlona and Delvina, situated opposite to Puglia, being now subject to the Porte, the reduction of this territory ought to be considered a matter of importance to the state. Kemal Reis, however, having recommended the capture of Corfu in the first place, the Sultan resolved upon going thither in person, and on a Friday, in the middle of Zilhijé 943 (May 1537), Lutfi Pasha being then commander of the fleet, Khair-ad-din sailed for the Mediterranean with one hundred and thirty-five galleys and other vessels, amounting in all to two hundred and eighty. Never before had so large a fleet sailed. Thirty thousand sailors had been collected from all parts of the Ottoman dominions. On the 7th of Zilhijé (17th May) the illustrious emperor with his two sons left the capital, and set out on his journey, taking Smako on the way.

* Literally " *rubbed his face against the royal stirrup.*"

About the end of Moharrem, 944 (A. D. 1533), they passed Albassan, and on the fifth of Seffer entered the plains of Avlona, where they had a sight of the royal fleet, which had arrived and lay off that coast.

The Vezier Mustaffa Pasha, having been charged with the subjugation of that part of Albania which was in rebellion, proceeded thither, and subdued it, plundering the inhabitants.   Avlona being bounded on the west by the sea, and on the east by rebellious Albania, the natives of which held intercourse with the infidel ships, by the advice of Eias Pasha the whole of that line of country was subjugated ; and the rebels of Delvina having also submitted, territory to the extent of two sanjaks was thus added to the Sublime Porte.

When the whole fleet was collected opposite Avlona, sixty vessels were consigned to Khair-ad-din to conduct those that were bringing provisions from Egypt. The chief commander, Lutfi Pasha, taking charge of the remaining vessels, went over to the Puglia coasts, and attacked a few castles, which he rased, first securing the prisoners and their wealth.

As Khair-ad-din was passing the island of Corfu, about forty Venetian galleys that were lying in the neighbourhood, seeing his fleet, and supposing that he was leaving altogether, resolved to join the rest of their fleet, which was then in the Gulf of Venice.   On their way to the rendezvous they were met by Lutfi Pasha on his return from Puglia, who gave them battle, sunk two of their ships, took two, and the rest escaped to Corfu.   Khair-ad-din then brought his provision-ships to Prevesa, and thence sailed to Avlona, where the sultan's fleet had again assembled.

ACCOUNT OF THE TREACHERY OF THE VENETIANS.

The Venetian infidels are a people famous for their great wealth, their extensive commerce, and their deceit and perfidy in all their transactions.   Having by treachery taken most of the islands in their possession from the Hungarian princes, and these islands being on the borders of the Ottoman dominions, and deriving their subsistence and trade from them, the Venetians from necessity maintain a show of friendship, but are in reality the most inveterate of all the enemies of the faith.   During the above expedition, they being unmolested, the governor of Gallipoli harbour, Ali Ketkhoda, happened to touch at Corfu with two galleys on his way to join the Moslem fleet, when Andrea Doria, who was there at the time, came out with the Corfiote vessels, and attacked him.   A fierce engagement ensued, in which the superior numbers of the infidels overcame the warriors, and the battle having lasted from morning till afternoon,[*] most of the Gallipoli vessels were burnt or sunk, and the survivors were made prisoners.

On another occasion, another governor of Gallipoli, Boustan Ketkhoda, was sailing to Corfu with dispatches from Lutfi Pasha, when four of the Venetian ships gave him chase, and captured him. It was of no avail that he declared he was only going on an embassy. Fearing however that the affair might become known, they sunk the vessel and cruelly murdered all that were on board, except a youth who threw himself into the sea, and floated on a board till he was taken up by one of the ships of the fleet, which conveyed him to Lutfi Pasha. Lutfi Pasha laid the matter before the Sultan, who, on account of these two outrages, commanded that Corfu should be besieged.

SIEGE OF CORFU.

Accordingly, the expedition to Puglia having been abandoned, the imperial fleet was ordered to lay siege to and plunder the castle of Corfu, whilst the emperor left Avlona, and took up his quarters over-against the island. According to one account, a bridge of boats was constructed across the channel where its width did not exceed half a mile, by means of which the armies of the faithful passed over to the island. One hundred and forty villages in the neighbourhood of the town were all pillaged, so that the town alone remained, against which the artillery was drawn up, and the siege was regularly commenced. But it being almost entirely surrounded by sea, they attacked it on the land side for full forty-three days and nights. When however they had opened the sally ports, and had several fierce engagements, they found their time for warlike operations was exhausted, the setting in of winter having commenced, and heavy rains falling, accompanied with extreme cold,—added to which, the sailing season was past. The emperor therefore, out of compassion for the army, sent Eias Pasha over to the island with orders to raise the siege. Lutfi Pasha and Khairad-din Pasha, however, remonstrated against this step, saying that so much labour ought not to be thrown away, and endeavoured to make the matter appear feasible : but there is an adage, " What is ordained must come to pass," and therefore their counsel did not meet the royal approbation. One history relates that when it was reported to his majesty that a cannon ball had killed four of his men, he declared he would not exchange one of his brave warriors for a

---

[*] Literally, " *the battle market having been kept hot from morning till afternoon.*"

thousand such castles, and immediately gave orders to raise the siege.   In short, the reduction of this place having been so long attempted without success, a divan was held about the end of the month Rabi-al-akher, and after robes of honor had been given to the nobles, presents to the naval capudans and reises, two pieces of money to each of the cavalry, and one piece to each of the infantry, on the 24th of the same month the troops retired from the siege, and his majesty, passing through Perpol, Kortsha, Prespa, Monaster, Florina, and Salonica, after a journey of twenty days, arrived at Adrianople.

Lutfi Pasha and Khair-ad-din Pasha on their return landed at Cephalonia, which they attacked and plundered, taking immense booty.

ATTACK OF KHAIR-AD-DIN UPON THE VENETIAN ISLANDS.

The royal fleet leaving Cephalonia proceeded to Motone, where Khair-ad-din chose sixty vessels, with which he remained at sea, Lutfi Pasha returning with the rest to the Porte.   Khair-ad-din first touched at Cerigo, whence he went to an island called Egina, which was a strong fortress.   To this, having prepared his artillery, he laid siege, and after three days' fighting, succeeded in capturing it on the fourth day, when he took four thousand eight hundred prisoners, besides considerable booty.   He then went to an island called Merted,* which he also took, and carried off twelve hundred prisoners.   He next proceeded to the island of Bara (Paros), which the infidels defended with great obstinacy for some time: but it was at length taken at the point of the sword, and yielded much plunder.   On his going against Naksha (Naxia), the infidels came out and agreed to an impost.   Khair-ad-din's men with his permission then went and plundered an island in the neighbourhood, and returned with great spoils. The victorious pasha then attacked another island, and in fourteen days took three of its castles and made eleven thousand prisoners.   Having done this, he bound down these six islands to pay an annual tribute of five thousand pieces of gold.   In the course of this expedition Khair-ad-din collected cloth, money, a thousand girls, and fifteen hundred boys—plunder amounting in all to the value of four hundred thousand pieces of gold : such at least was the calculation of his wealth.   He then returned to Constantinople.

* *Merted*, probably Zea.

THE CAPUDAN PASHA'S PRESENT TO THE SULTAN.

The morning after his arrival the pasha dressed two hundred boys in scarlet, bearing in their hands flasks and goblets of gold and silver.   Behind them followed thirty others, each carrying on his shoulders a purse of gold ; after these came two hundred men, each carrying a purse of money ; and lastly, two hundred infidels wearing collars, each bearing a roll of cloth on his back.   These he took as a present to the emperor, and having kissed the royal hand, was presented with robes of the most splendid kind, and received the highest marks of honour ; for never at any period had any capudan done such signal service.

THIRD EXPEDITION OF KHAIR-AD-DIN PASHA.

The winter season being nearly over, Sultan Soleiman gave orders to his veziers to equip a hundred and fifty vessels, and to send Khair-ad-din to sea.   Accordingly, although the ships were not ready, the veziers pressed Khair-ad-din to sail ; and he not consenting, they had recourse to stratagem, saying that Andrea Doria had gone with forty vessels to Candia, where he was waiting to intercept Saleh Reis, who with twenty vessels had gone to bring the Indian merchandise from Egypt.   Khair-ad-din therefore with the forty ships that were in readiness (the other ninety being ordered to follow) sailed on the ninth of Moharrem, 945, (June 8th, 1538,) accompanied by three thousand janissaries ; and Ali Beg, the beg of Kogia-eili, Khorrem Beg, the beg of Tekké, Ali Beg, the beg of Seida, and Mustaffa Beg, the beg of Alanieh, having joined him, they proceeded to Imbro, where some time previously a vessel containing seventeen pieces of cannon had been wrecked, and having possessed themselves of these, they sailed to an island called Ishkatos (Skiathos), which had a strong castle and harbour. In consequence of the complaint of the governor of Negropont that the pirates were in the habit of lying there and carrying on their depredations in the vicinity, they conveyed their artillery from a distance of seven miles, and blockaded the castle for six days and nights, taking it by assault on the seventh day.   A great number of the infidels were slain, and three thousand eight hundred taken prisoners.

The ninety vessels from Constantinople, and Saleh Reis, with the twenty under his command, had now arrived ; so that, according to the royal command, the fleet now consisted of a hundred and fifty vessels ; but the equipment and manning of the ninety from the Porte not being quite complete, Khair-ad-din emptied and sent back twelve of them to Gallipoli; the rest he despatched to the Negropont. The fleet then touched at Eskeri (Skyro), which they left the same night. In the forenoon of the following day, which was very foggy, they met seventy of the Mediterranean pirate boats which had but the day before attempted in vain to take Skyro. On the approach of Khair-ad-din, however, the infidels of the castle surrendered, crying for quarter; and he accordingly spared them, on the condition that they should pay an annual sum of one thousand pieces of gold. At this place he remained a short time, and oiled his vessels. With the plunder he took he filled seven vessels, and sent them to Constantinople. Two cannoniers had been sent from Candia to Skyro; but not arriving till the afternoon, when the castle had surrendered, they were seized and brought before the pasha, who having obtained from them the information he needed respecting the enemy's movements, divided his fleet into seven squadrons, which he sent in different directions,—one cruising about the islands to levy the tribute. He then sailed to Istandil (Tino), the governor of which was a Frank, and the people Greeks. These immediately surrendered, and the pasha agreed to molest them no further if they would deliver up their chiefs, which they accordingly did. He then appointed one of the principal inhabitants governor, and stipulated for an annual tribute of five thousand pieces of gold. He next sailed to Andro, the people of which also submitted. On this and a neighbouring island he imposed an annual tribute of one thousand pieces of gold. From Andro the squadron proceeded to Naxia, and received the tribute from that island, the inhabitants firing a salute. In the afternoon of the third day from this time, as they were sailing to Candia, they perceived before them a huge barge, which seemed like a black mountain rising out of the sea. They immediately bore down upon her; but she received their fire for a considerable time without striking her colours. At length, however, she was weakened by several balls striking her prow, when the Capudan Ibrahim went in and took her in tow. On the fifteenth of Seffer the fleet arrived at Candia, first touching at the castle of Miloietimo, where they landed their men. They then plundered twenty of the neighbouring villages, which had been abandoned by the infidels, and proceeding thence to Bakorna, took the natives prisoners, and plundered sixty of the adjacent villages. On the 17th they sailed towards a very strong castle called Khania (Canea), and as the infidels had fled into the fortress, took in a supply of water, and made preparations to attack it. But several of the more experienced capudans were of opinion that to attack this castle would be a most difficult matter; because, being on the side next the sea strongly fortified, and on the land side protected by a wall of three miles in extent, besides being well stored with arms and ammunition, and strongly garrisoned, to effect its reduction would require an armament of no ordinary strength.   For these reasons they desisted from their attack, but fired the houses on the outside, demolished all the strong buildings in the neighbourhood, and in the course of three days plundered three hundred villages.   They then came upon Menolilo and Retimo, the villages of which they plundered.   Thence they went to Ista (Setia), where the inhabitants seemed disposed to resist: but finding themselves unable to hold out, speedily took to flight.   Most of them were taken prisoners, and the rest were devoured by the sword.   Two castles, called Isklaria and Istilo, were next reduced, and eighty villages in their neighbourhood plundered.   In one short week the whole of Candia was overrun and pillaged.   More than fifteen thousand prisoners were taken, of whom a few were sent in barges to Constantinople. The fleet afterwards proceeded to the island of Kirpé, which had three forts. Here they remained ten days, during which they took all the three, and laid them under tribute.

The heat at this time became very oppressive, and hot winds like the Sam* beginning to blow, and the sailors suffering much, the fleet went over to the island of Ilki (Piscopia), where they rested for some time.   Sailing thence to Stanko, they broke up the levend frigates, and manned the galleys with the sailors they found on board.   Besides these, they also took in a great number of infidel sailors from the islands and the Anatolian coasts.   They then reduced an island called Stanpalia, which the pasha left to be plundered by the volunteer ships.   This year the Venetians possessed twenty-five islands, each having one, two, or three castles; all of which were taken; twelve of the islands being laid under tribute, and the remaining thirteen plundered.

After this the fleet sailed towards Roumelia, and having broken up the heavy sailing vessels at Kuzil Hissar, put into the harbour of Negropont.   They then took over the light sailing vessels by night to Kara-Ata, where they oiled their sides, and returned to Negropont to take in provisions.   At this time Saleh Reis, who was a most valiant commander, arrived at Negropont with thirty vessels; on which occasion numerous salutes were fired.

THE GRAND BATTLE OF KHAIR-AD-DIN PASHA.

About this time information was received that the Spanish, Papal, and Venetian fleets had assembled at Corfu, and attacked Prevesa; whereupon Khair-ad-din

* *Sam*, a sort of Simmoom.

sent twenty small privateers to that quarter, which, on reaching Zante, came in sight of forty guard ships. These latter immediately returned to their fleet and gave information that Barbarossa was in the neighbourhood. The enemy then left Prevesa; which circumstance being made known to Khair-ad-din, when he was near Motone, he took in water at Helomej, and proceeded thence to Cephalonia, where he landed his men and plundered the surrounding villages. Crossing thence to Prevesa, the castle of which had been much injured by the enemy's cannon, he was preparing to besiege it, when he received reinforcements during the night from Santa Maura. With this assistance he entered the fortress, many of the infidels being slain in the assault : and having planted his great guns, the infidels, exhausted and terrified, left the place.* The pasha then ordered his troops to repair the fortress; and in the mean time sent over a few private vessels to the infidel coasts to obtain information. These on their return reported that the Spanish, Papal, Portuguese and Venetian fleets had assembled at Corfu. This intelligence was immediately forwarded to the sultan, who was then on an expedition into Boghdan (Moldavia). About the middle of the month Jemazi-al-avul the fleets of these accursed infidels arrived and anchored about two miles from Prevesa.

THE NUMBER OF THE INFIDELS' SHIPS.

Andrea Doria had fifty-two galleys; the Venetian general, seventy; the Pope's admiral, thirty; and the lieutenant of the Grand-Master of Rhodes, ten. The Spaniards and Portuguese had eighty barges, and the Venetians ten krakas, each of which contained two thousand arms of different sorts, and was equal to fifty galleys. Andrea Doria's own ship was a huge galleon, with arms and ammunition beyond computation. Besides these there were a few barges from different places; the whole amounting to one hundred and sixty-two galleys, one hundred and forty barges, and three hundred other ships, which, with the small privateers, formed a fleet of upwards of six hundred sail.

The Moslem fleet consisted of only one hundred and twenty-two light galleys. Khair-ad-din having held a consultation, and encouraged his troops, began to make preparations for an engagement. He then lowered the masts, giving strict injunctions to his officers to keep a constant eye upon his movements. The private vessels he ordered to take a position by themselves out of the line, and when

---

* According to Rycaut, Prevesa had just been taken by the Patriarch Grimmanus, who had the command of the Pope's galleys. The grand fleet had left this place before Khair-ad-din's arrival.

they came in contact with the enemy's ships to fire their bow-guns. The begs, seeing the number of the infidel ships, recommended the landing of the men and artillery. Khair-ad-din however did not consider this advisable; but having afterwards ascertained that the plan of the enemy was to enter the bay of Prevesa by night, he landed his men and stationed his artillery on the shore. The infidels shortly afterwards landed, when he commenced a fire upon them, whilst Mourad Agha, of the line of privateers, Tourghoudjé, Kouzloujé Mohammed, Sadek Reis, and several others, attacked them in the rear, and filled them with terror. Two days after several of the enemy's light vessels came up to the strait of Prevesa, where the arrogant wretches opened a fire upon the Moslem vessels. The brave and experienced pasha, unable to bear this insolence any longer, beat his drum and cymbals, hoisted his flags, and sailed out of the bay, with the intention of there meeting the fleet of the despicable infidels. Casting anchor about six miles from land, he waited until the rest of the Moslem vessels should join him; and when they were all assembled, and had taken their proper positions, gave a signal, at which each of the hundred and twenty-two ships fired three guns, and coming forward to the attack, the brave Moslems filled the air with their shouts. This struck dismay into the hearts of the infidels, who, as evening approached, weighed anchor and fled towards Corfu. The pasha then returned to his former position. That night, whilst praying for direction, he saw in a dream great numbers of fishes issuing out of the harbour; and rising up at midnight, he sailed in that direction.

ATTACK AND FLIGHT OF THE INFIDELS.

On the third of Jemazi-al-avul, as Andrea Doria was preparing to enter the Gulf of Lepanto, Khair-ad-din sailed to Bahshiler, and having reached that place, he sent men to the mast-heads, who descried masts in the neighbourhood of Santa Maura and the harbour of Ingir. He therefore immediately weighed anchor, and sailed, prepared for an engagement. The infidels observing them, came out to meet them; and the wind being in their favour, the Moslems were overwhelmed with fear, for galleys are not able to compete with barges under such circumstances. Khair-ad-din however wrote two verses of the Koran, and threw one on each side of his vessel; when the wind immediately fell, and the barges lay motionless. This occurrence teaches that commanders, however celebrated, ought not to trust in human means alone, but also to pay all possible regard to spiritual means for ensuring success. The unfortunate infidels, stationing themselves in regular lines, now began to discharge their artillery; which, however, wanted

strength to make it efficient. A galleon first came out and opened a heavy fire, but
was driven back by the fire of the fleet. Khair-ad-din succeeded in taking several of
the barges by attacking them from a distance, and thus gradually weakening them.
Andrea Doria and the general having now come up with their galleys, were about
to commence an attack, when the brave pasha bore down upon them, and commenced a heavy fire, which obliged them to bring round their barges. The balls
from the barges now fell like rain, and the two fleets were so enveloped in smoke,
that they could not see each other. The enemy's galleys several times attempted
to take the Moslem vessels in the rear, that so they might take up a position between them and the other ships and barges. The latter, which, from their size re-
sembled floating castles, were dashing against each other with great violence ; nor
was it possible to separate them. At length, after nine of the barges had been
driven back by the strength of the Moslem vessels, the pasha (of lion-like courage) redoubled his exertions, and keeping up a brisk fire, sunk several, and
clearing a way through them, passed on to the galleys, strictly prohibiting his men
from plundering a single barge. The infidels were astonished, and overwhelmed
with terror at the impetus of the warriors : and their small galleys being unable
any longer to maintain the fight, they turned their faces to flight. The slaughter
continued during the whole of the interval between the two hours of prayer, and
most of the barges were either destroyed or sunk by the cannon. Andrea Doria
seeing this tore his beard, and took to flight, all the smaller galleys following him.
The Moslems, supposing the barges were of less value than the galleys, pursued
the latter, and succeeded in capturing two of them.

In the evening the wind fell, which obliged them to remain on the scene of
action ; whilst the unfortunate infidels set fire to the remaining barges, which continued to burn till morning. Such wonderful battles as those fought between
the forenoon and sunset of that day were never before seen at sea.

Next morning the pasha went to Santa Maura, where he gave his son charge of
two captains he had taken, and despatched him to the sultan with the news of
the victory. He then proceeded to Prevesa, where the begs kissed his hand and
congratulated him. Sultan Soleiman Khan was at this time hunting at Ianboli,
where the pasha's son on his arrival was received with the greatest honors ; and
a divan being assembled, the proclamation of the victory was read, all present
standing, and thanksgiving and praise were offered to the Divine Being. The
Capudan Pasha then received orders to make an advance of one hundred thousand pieces of money to the principal officers, to send the proclamation of the
victory to all parts of the country, and to order public rejoicings in all the
towns.

Andrea Doria after his flight made Corfu his place of rendezvous ; whilst the pasha on the 14th of the same month started from Prevesa by night, and on the evening of the following day arrived at Bahshiler; but finding no traces of the infidels there, he returned to Prevesa. The privateers having obtained his permission to plunder Cephalonia, proceeded thither, and left nothing behind them but the bare fortress. On the other hand, whilst the pasha was engaged in repairing the fortress of Prevesa, information was brought him that the infidels had attacked Durazzo; upon which he cleared his galleys, and stood out to sea the same night. Next morning he attacked the fort of Parga, put the inhabitants to flight, took four hundred prisoners, and plundered and set fire to the castle. On his way to Bahshiler he took two barges; and after resting there two days, on the morning of the third, he again sailed to the channel of Corfu, where he was overtaken by a violent storm, which obliged him to put into Avlona, where he was detained for ten days till the weather cleared up. During this time the army suffered greatly. While there the pasha received orders either to winter there, or to return to Constantinople, as he might think most advisable. He chose the latter alternative, and immediately sailed for Constantinople. On their way the fleet had to encounter another dreadful storm at the strait of Beberjek, but succeeded in reaching Gallipoli, and thence proceeded to Constantinople, which they entered amidst the firing of numerous salutes.

CAPTURE OF CASTEL NOVO BY THE INFIDELS.

Andrea, taking advantage of the storm which detained Khair-ad-din at Avlona, returned and attacked Novo; and the governor being a weak man, he with the most consummate assurance took possession of it, garrisoned it with six thousand soldiers, and left it.

EXPEDITION OF SOLEIMAN PASHA TO INDIA.

Spain had just completed the conquest of the New World; and so early as the year 900 (A. D. 1494.) the Portuguese, emboldened by her success, proceeded from the Western to the Eastern Ocean, and passing along the Mountains of the Moon, (where the blessed Nile has its source,) and the coasts of Abyssinia and Zanguebar, penetrated into India, and took possession of the fortresses of Sind. The kings of that country being too weak to resist them, the king of Guzerat applied for assistance to Sultan Soleiman Khan. This zealous monarch, with the

ι

view of driving the oppressive infidels from the coasts of Yemen and India, equipped a fleet of thirty galleys in the road of Suez, and gave the command of them to Khadem Soleiman Pasha, chief of the emirs of Egypt, who left the port of Suez about the end of Moharrem (940 A. D. 1533), and arrived on the seventh of Rabi-al-avul at the city of Aden, on the coast of Yemen, the fortresses of which, under the command of Amar Ben Davud, he took possession of, and having considerably strengthened them, gave them in charge to Behram Beg. He then proceeded towards Div, an Indian port in the possession of the Portuguese, which was the principal object of his efforts. The winds being favourable, he arrived in the beginning of Rabi-al-avul at the citadels of Goa and Kari, situate in the neighbourhood of Div, and also in the possession of the Portuguese, where he landed his men and artillery, and took both these fortresses; a thousand infidels falling by the sword. He next laid siege to Div, the citadel of which was defended on three sides by the sea, and on the land side by very strong fortifications; on which account he deemed it advisable to land twenty thousand men, and a considerable quantity of ammunition. The siege had now lasted a month, and the king of Guzerat had in vain expected the ammunition and provisions he had demanded from Prince Mahmoud. This prince, frightened at the murder of Amar, the emir of Aden, would neither come himself nor send succours. The besieged infidels then, as a last resource, persuaded Mahmoud that the murder was committed by Soleiman Pasha, and that any good the latter might do him would be dictated by treachery. Deceived by these insinuations of the infidels, he decidedly refused the succours. This refusal, together with his open opposition to them in other matters, and the peace he had made with the infidels, obliged the Moslems to raise the siege of the citadel: and they accordingly reimbarked their artillery and departed for Shedjer, where they arrived safely in twenty days. The governor of this city having surrendered, the fleet departed for Aden and Zebid. Emir Ahmed, having taken possession of the country, was then its governor. On the approach of Soleiman, the emir shut himself up in a fortress, which was subsequently taken, and the command of the province of Yemen was given to Mustafa Beg, son of Mohammed Pasha Bikli.* Soleiman Pasha, after remaining a month at these places for the defence of Yemen, sailed for Jidda, where he arrived on the twentieth of Sheval. Immediately on his arrival there he undertook the pilgrimage (to Mecca), and whilst the fleet continued its voyage, accompanying the caravan, he proceeded by land to Egypt, and at length reached Constantinople, where he obtained a seat in the divan.

* *Bikli,* "the moustached."

EXPEDITION OF KHAIR-AD-DIN TO CASTEL NOVO.

The recovery of Castel Novo, which some time before had fallen into the hands of the infidels, being considered a matter of importance both to religion and the state, on the return of spring Khosrow Pasha, the begler-beg of Roumelia, who had remained at Sophia, was sent thither by land. Khair-ad-din also, on the eighth of Rabi-al-akher, sailed with one hundred and fifty vessels, and with thirty-seven pieces of cannon besieged the fortress. After a discharge of eight thousand two hundred shots, on the twenty-second day the walls of one of the fortresses were reduced and the fortress itself taken. Novo had two large fortresses; they therefore proceeded to the other one, which they also took by assault, making the infidels prisoners. The pasha then rebuilt the castle, and placed twenty-six pieces of cannon in it. He then sent his troops to plunder the country of the infidels, and returned to Constantinople with immense riches.

ATTACK OF THE KING OF SPAIN UPON ALGIERS, &c.

In the year 948 (A. D. 1541) the emperor went with his army on an expedition into Hungary, and sent Khair-ad-din at the same time with seventy galleys to guard the Mediterranean. At this time too, the king of Spain, in order to assist the emperor Ferdinand, and to plunder the Moslem territories, sailed with his fleet towards the Venetian coasts. When he heard that Khair-ad-din was at sea, ashamed to return to his own country, he proceeded to Algiers. For some time previous to this Khadem Hassan Agha, to whose care the pasha had confided Algiers, having equipped thirty galleys and golettas, had been carrying on a system of plunder on the Spanish coasts. The king of Spain therefore embarked troops to the number of fifty thousand, four thousand of which were cavalry, on board a hundred galleys, and sailed for Algiers, where he arrived on the twenty-eighth day of Jemazi II., A. H. 948. Hassan thereupon immediately held a divan, and encouraged his men. Meantime the infidels had pitched their camp, and were attempting a trench, when Hassan Beg, with six hundred Turkish and two thousand Arab horsemen, sallied out and attacked them by night. In the confusion which ensued and the darkness of the night the infidels fell upon each other, and three thousand of them were killed; and the warriors returned in safety to the castle.   By the decree of God, on the fifth day there was a violent storm of wind and rain, which drove most of the enemy's heavy barges ashore, and sunk several; their ammunition too was wet, and their cannon and musketry unfit for service.   Hassan Beg therefore made an attack upon them, and after a hot engagement of two hours, returned to the castle.   In this storm a hundred and six of the infidels' ships were driven ashore, and four galleys into the harbour.   In these were one thousand four hundred Moslem prisoners, who were immediately liberated.   The infidels, mortified and disappointed, now retired and assembled at a cape called Tementos, whence they set out on their return to their own country.   They were pursued by the Moslems, who slew great numbers of them : whilst the Algerines, observing the violence of the stream of dissension which was strongly agitated among them, plunged into it, and sunk or destroyed many of their ships.   Those who escaped embarked on board the remaining vessels, and on the 26th of Rajab again put out to sea, but were again overtaken by a storm, which drove them to Bajaiah, and at length with great difficulty made their way to Spain.   Not long after this memorable defeat by the storm, which is recorded in the Spanish histories, Charles V. entered a monastery and became a recluse; and his kingdom passed to his son.

FRANCE CRAVES ASSISTANCE OF THE PORTE.

In the year 949 Francis king of France sent an ambassador to the Sublime Porte, to request the aid of a naval force and other assistance, in consequence of a terrible feud that existed between him and Spain.   Orders having been given this winter to fit out a considerable number of vessels, Khair-ad-din, in compliance with this request, equipped a hundred galleys, and in the spring of the year 950 sailed with a complete fleet for France.   Several historical accounts agree in this statement.   On this occasion victory deserted the arms of the pasha.

DEATH OF KHAIR-AD-DIN PASHA.

The pasha, after remaining at sea two years longer, to protect its navigation, returned to the Porte, where he died on the sixth of Jemazi-al-avul, 953

(A. D. August 1546), upwards of eighty years old, and was buried in his tomb at Beshektash.   The period of his death is chronogrammatically expressed in the sentence,* "The chief of the sea is dead."   May the mercy of God be extended to him!

---

* The numerical value of مات ريٰس البحر is 953.

CHAPTER IV.

Of the Expeditions of the Capudans from the time of Khair-ad-din Pasha till that of Pialeh Pasha.

THE EXPEDITIONS OF MOHAMMED PASHA.

AFTER the death of Khair-ad-din Pasha, the vezier Mohammed Pasha was made capudan, and held that office for two or three years, when he was presented with the governorship of Roumelia. He was afterwards appointed grand vezier, and performed the functions of that office at Scutari.

THE CAPTURE OF TRIPOLI BY SENAN PASHA.

On Mohammed Pasha's being made capudan he went on an expedition against Tripoli (West), which was formerly in the possession of the Tunisian kings, the Beni Hefs: but about A. H. 916 (A. D. 1510) the Spaniards, taking advantage of the supineness of the reigning monarch, Mohammed Ben Hassan, the nineteenth king of that dynasty, who was immersed in pleasure, captured the castles of Vahran, Bajaiah and Tripoli. The last of these places had now been forty-two years in their possession, when his majesty, wishing to reduce it, invited Tourghoudjé Beg, (who formerly had the sanjak of Karli-Eili [Acarnania], but had now on some account gone to Moghreb, where he remained two years,) under whose direction Senan Pasha, A. H. 958 (A.D. 1551) sailed with twenty galleys, and besieged and took the castle. Tourghoudjé Beg had been promised the governorship of it for his life, but Senan Pasha gave it to Khadem Mourad Agha. Tourghoudjé Beg, however, subsequently received it from the emperor in person, and held it till he was murdered at Malta eleven years afterwards.

EXPEDITION OF PIRI REIS TO THE EASTERN OCEAN.

Notwithstanding Soleiman Pasha had, when he reduced Aden, left a garrison in that city, the people joined the Portuguese, the masters of India, turned away their faces from submission, and delivered up the fortress to the infidels. To recover it, Piri Pasha, the capudan of Egypt, (son of the sister of Kemal Reis, and author of the Bahria,*) was sent from Suez with a fleet ; and leaving the Red Sea, proceeded by the straits of Babelmandel to Aden, against the fortress of which he planted his artillery, and having taken it by storm, left in it a considerable garrison provided with the necessary means of defence. Davoud Pasha, the governor of Egypt, having represented to the sultan the importance of the service rendered by Piri Reis, the latter received in recompense lands to the value of one hundred thousand aspres.

SECOND EXPEDITION OF PIRI PASHA TO THE EASTERN OCEAN.

Piri Pasha, the capudan of Egypt, left Suez A. H. 959 with a fleet of thirty sail, consisting of galleys, bashderdés, golettas, and galleons; and proceeding to Aden by Jedda and Babelmandel, sailed thence towards Ras-al-had, passing Zaffar and Shedjer. On his route he was overtaken near Shedjer by a storm, in which several of his barges were destroyed. With the remains of his fleet he attacked Muscat, a fortress in the Persian Gulf, in the country of Oman, which he took, and made the inhabitants prisoners. He then laid waste the islands of Ormuz and Barkhet. On his arrival at Bassora he heard that the fleet of the vile infidels was advancing towards him; a report which was confirmed by the infidel capudan whom he took at Muscat, and who now advised him to remain no longer in his present situation, on account of the impossibility of escaping by the strait of Ormuz. The pasha, being unable to clear the whole of his fleet, departed before the arrival of the infidels, with three galleys, his private property. One of these he lost near Bahrein, and with the remaining two returned to Egypt. Of the vessels left at Bassora, Kobad Pasha, the governor of

---

* A work on navigation, of which further mention is made below, p. 72.

that city, offered the command to Ali Beg, a beg of Egypt, and a commander in the army ; who, however, refused it, and returned by land to Egypt: and the vessels, thus abandoned, were soon destroyed. The pasha of Egypt, apprised of these events, seized and imprisoned Piri Reis on his arrival at Cairo, and sent information of the circumstance to the Sublime Porte, whence he immediately received an order to put to death the admiral, who was beheaded accordingly in the divan of Cairo. He left immense riches, which were confiscated to the treasury. The inhabitants of Ormuz, from whom he had extorted large sums of money, came to complain of his exactions and crave an indemnity ; but no attention was paid to their demands, and the gold was put into gilt vases and sent to Constantinople. Piri Reis composed a work on navigation, in which he has given a description of the Mediterranean. This is the only work of the kind of any authority amongst the Moslems.

EXPEDITION OF MURAD PASHA TO INDIA.

The Sublime Porte now entrusted the command of the fleet to Murad Beg formerly governor of the sanjak of Katif, and ordered him to remain at Bassora, with the vessels already in his command, consisting of five galleys and one goletta. Shortly after, he quitted Bassora, at the head of a fleet of fifteen galleys and two barges, (one of his galleys having sunk,) and directed his course towards Egypt. Near Ormuz he met the infidels' fleet, which he immediately attacked, and a desperate engagement ensued, in which Soleiman Reis, (the Capudan Reis,) Rajab Reis, with a great number of men, obtained the palm of martyrdom, and many others were wounded. The infidels did considerable damage to the Moslem ships, which, unable to sustain the continual fire of the enemy, escaped by night. One of their vessels, which was left behind, was driven ashore near Lar, and captured by the infidels, part of the crew escaping and the rest being made prisoners. The remainder of the fleet returned to Bassora, whence tidings of the sad event were immediately communicated to the Sublime Porte.

ACCOUNT OF SEIDI ALI, CAPUDAN.

Seidi Ali Ibn Hosein, whose poetical appellation was Katebi, besides being famed for his poetical productions, was celebrated for his works on navigation and astronomy, as well in prose as in verse. He was author of a work called

Mohit, (the Ocean,) on the Indian Ocean, and of another called the *Merat-al Kainat*, (the Mirror of Creation,) treating of the science of the astrolabe, of squares, circles, and sines. He was moreover the translator of a work called the Fat'hia. There has never been his equal in the arsenal. He served with the late sultan, Soleiman Khan, at the capture of Rhodes, and afterwards in Moghreb, and other places with Khair-ad-din Pasha, Senan Pasha, and many others. His father and grandfather having held the office of governor of the arsenal ever since the capture of Constantinople, the science of navigation descended to him as a legacy; and it was on this account that Sultan Soleiman Khan, about the end of the year 960 (A. D. 1553), rewarded him with the post of capudan of Egypt, and ordered him to bring to Cairo the vessels which were lying at Bassora.

EXPEDITION OF SEIDI ALI TO THE EASTERN OCEAN.

In the month of Moharrem (December), A. H. 961 (A. D. 1553), the Capudan Seidi Ali, following the orders he had received, left Aleppo and proceeded to Bassora by way of Mousul and Baghdad. Favourable winds now began to blow, and the capudan, in order to avail himself of them, hastened to equip the five* barges that were lying there. Mustapha Pasha, the governor of Bassora, and a distinguished seaman, was absent from the city when Seidi Ali arrived; having been ordered by the Porte to sail with a frigate to Ormuz, and was at this moment on his way thither. Being informed that the infidels had only four ships, he immediately communicated the intelligence to Seidi Ali, who thereupon embarked his troops and quitted Bassora early in the month of Shaban (July), and joined Mustapha Pasha near Ormuz. Passing Abadan, Desboul, and Shutar, and coasting Harek and Katif in the neighbourhood of Lahsa, they arrived at Bahrein, where they had an interview with the governor, Murad Reis. Here the sailors, by sinking leathern bottles about eight fathoms into the sea obtained fresh water. They sailed hence to old Ormuz, Barkhet and Ormuz; after which the sherif Mustapha returned to the Porte. Seidi Ali then passed the coast of Zaffar, and early on the morning of the fortieth day, which was the tenth of Ramazan, met the infidels near the city of Khourfekan. Their fleet consisted of four immense barges, three large galleons, six Portuguese guard-ships, and twelve golettas.

---

* If these are the barges mentioned at p. 72, this should of course be read *fifteen.*

K

THE ENGAGEMENT BETWEEN SEIDI ALI AND THE PORTUGUESE.

The Moslems immediately hoisted their colours, weighed anchor, and got in readiness all their warlike machines. With flags hoisted and sails spread, and looking in confidence to the Supreme Being, they set up Mohammedan shouts, and commenced an attack, the fierceness of which baffles description. By the favour of God, their fire struck one of the Portuguese galleons, which was wrecked on the island of Fak-al-asad. They fought bravely till night-fall, when the capudan hoisted the lights. The infidels however fired a gun as the signal of retreat, and fled to Ormuz. Thus, by the favour of God, the victory was left to the Moslems, who, favoured by the winds, departed next day for the city of Khour-fekan, where the troops took in a supply of fresh water, and after seventeen days' sailing, arrived in the neighbourhood of Muscat and Kalat.

SECOND EXPEDITION OF SEIDI ALI, AGAINST THE CAPUDAN OF GOA.

On the morning of the 26th of Ramazan the captain of Goa, the son of the governor, left the harbour of Muscat, and with his barges, guard-ships, and galleons, with their mainsails spread and colours flying, sailed against the Moslems, who, still trusting in God, remained near the shore prepared for battle.

The enemy's barges first came up, and attacked the galleys, when a sharp fire was opened on both sides, and a furious engagement ensued. The infidels then began to shower down their hand-grenades from the maintops upon the galleys, one of which and a barge which was near it they burnt by throwing a bomb into the galley. Five barges and as many galleys were driven ashore and lost. Another barge was driven ashore by the violence with which the wind beat against it, and was lost. At length the sailors and the troops on both sides were exhausted, the former being unable to pull at the oars, and the latter to work the guns any longer; they were therefore obliged to cast anchor: but even in this position they fought for some time with springs to their cables. They were finally obliged to abandon their boats. Elmshah Reis, Kara Mustaffa, and Kalfat Mumi, the commanders of the lost galleys, and Durzi Mustaffa Beg, the commander of the volunteers, with about two hundred Egyptian soldiers, reached the shore in safety, and afterwards returned to the fleet, bringing with them many Arabs to the assistance of the Moslems. The infidels also recovered the men who were in their barges which had been driven ashore. This battle was even greater than that between Khair-ad-din and Andrea Doria. Few soldiers are known to have ever been engaged in such a fight. At last, when night approached, a strong gale began to blow, and each of the barges threw out two stream anchors; but the men on board were so overcome with fatigue, that they were obliged to stand out from the shore, and sail before the wind. In this way they came to the coast of Barjash, where, finding plenty of sea, they succeeded in reaching Bender Shehbar in Mekran. Here they took in water, and by the direction of a pilot, reached Bender Goader; the governor of which, Malek Dinar Oghli Jelal-ad-din, came to examine the state of their fleet, and represented to the sultan the necessity of sending supplies: in consequence of which, fifty or sixty vessels with provisions were sent out, and joined them before they reached Ormuz.

THE RESULT OF SEIDI ALI'S EXPEDITION TO THE INDIAN OCEAN.

From Bender Goader the capudan again sailed with nine vessels for the Indian Ocean, and directed his course towards Yemen. For a few days the weather was favourable, and they had arrived in the neighbourhood of Zaffar and Shedjer, when the westerly winds began to blow, and they were overtaken by the storm called *the Elephant*, before which they scudded, being unable even to carry the foresail. Compared with this, a storm in the Mediterranean is as insignificant as a grain of sand: day could not be distinguished from night, and the waves rose like huge mountains. Their vessels were thus greatly injured, and they were obliged to throw overboard a great part of their ammunition and stores. In this way they drifted before the wind for ten days, during which time it rained incessantly, and there was no appearance of daylight. The sailors here saw immense fishes, of the length of two galleys; at which their spirits rose, because they consider them animals of good omen. They also saw sea-horses, huge serpents, tortoises as large as millstones, and sea-weed. After having been detained a long time, they at last approached the bay of Chekd.

ACCOUNT OF A WHIRLPOOL.

Suddenly the colour of the sea became changed to a whitish hue, and the sailors began to cry out. The cause of their alarm was what in the Indian Ocean is called a whirlpool, a thing very common about Gerdefoon on the Ethiopian coast, and in the bay of Chekd near Sind. It is stated in maritime works that ships getting into one of these must inevitably perish. Having sounded, and found they had only five fathoms water, they took in their sails. Towards morning the wind fell a little, and they sent up an able seaman to the mast-head, who descried a temple on the land. Soon after they passed Kormian, Mangalore, and Somnat, and came very near Div; but the latter place being in the hands of the infidels, they did not show their sail that day, but made the best of their way. Again the wind increased, and the helms became quite unmanageable: the boat-swain's whistle could not be distinguished from the whistling of the wind, and no one could walk the decks. They were also obliged to shut up most of the troops in the holds. In short, the horrors of this day were comparable only to those of the resurrection. At length they reached the coast of Guzerat, in India, when the sailors suddenly cried out that a hurricane was before them ; upon which they dropped anchor ; but the sea was so heavy that the ships were nearly upset. The galley-slaves broke their chains, and all the men, stripping themselves naked, began to provide themselves with barrels and leathern bottles for their escape. some of the anchors, however, broke ; and thus the vessels escaped the hurricane. This occurred at a place between Div and Daman. Towards afternoon the weather became somewhat fairer, which enabled them to proceed to the port of Daman in the district of Guzerat, where they anchored about two miles from the shore. For five days the hurricane continued to blow with great violence, and was ac-companied with incessant rains. The vessels had now shipped much water ; and three of them, losing their anchorage, drifted ashore ; but all on board landed in safety. When the storm had somewhat abated, they succeeded in gaining the harbour of Daman, where they gave the guns and ammunition of the wrecked vessels in charge to Malek Asad, governor of Daman, and one of the emirs of Sultan Ahmed, the king of Guzerat. Malek Asad then cautioned them not to go to the castle of Sert, as the fleet of the infidels was about to attack it. Hearing this, most of the men, who had already suffered such hardships, landed, and entered the service of Malek Asad ; whilst others of them, after heaping reproaches on the capudan, seized the boats, in which they reached the shore, and proceeded overland to Sert. Seidi Ali, with the remaining vessels and men, directed his course to Sert, which, sometimes sailing, and sometimes availing himself of the assistance of the oars, he reached in five days: a period of three months, in which he underwent thousands of difficulties, having elapsed since he left Bassora. The Moslems at this place were rejoiced to see them, for the country of Guzerat was at this time in a very disturbed state. Here also several untoward events befell them : the supplies for the troops were exhausted ; the ammunition and stores of the vessels were consumed ; the vessels themselves were much injured ; and their return to Egypt was considered quite impossible. Under these circumstances, most of the men entered the service of the king of Guzerat, and the ships were left empty. The capudan, having received from the governor of Sert, an undertaking that the value of the arms and other effects which were left with him should be sent to the Sublime Porte, set out by land for Constantinople on the first of Moharrem, A. H. 962 (A. D. 26th November, 1554), accompanied by fifty attendants. Having travelled through India and Persia, after an absence of four years, he arrived at Constantinople in the month of Rajab, 964 (A. D. May, 1557). Shortly afterwards he was admitted to the royal presence at Adrianople, and had an addition of eighty aspres made to his salary; whilst all his companions were promoted in Egypt; and the royal order was issued that they should be paid their four years' salary which was in arrear. The capudan then wrote an account of his voyages and travels, which he entitled, "The Adventures of Seidi Ali." From this work the foregoing particulars are extracted.

THE EXPEDITION OF SENAN PASHA.

In 959 the Capudan Senan Pasha went to sea with one hundred and twenty vessels, the command of which he held till the end of 960. He died in 961, and was buried at Scutari. The poet Sahari has thus commemorated the period of his death:

Fate at last gives up the body to decay, even should it be that of Noah the pilot.

Whenever the huge leviathan Death draws a breath, the ocean seems but a drop to him.

To his friends Senan was another Joseph; to his enemies he was a dart.

Come, Sahari, let us offer up a prayer for him; "May God make glad his pure spirit!"

The invisible Spirit has revealed the time of his death. "The capudan has joined the Divine Mercy."

THE APPEARANCE OF TORGHUDJEH BEG.

Torghudjeh was the son of a rayah called Veli, and was born at a village in the neighbourhood of Seroloz, of the sanjak of Mantesheh. Being of a brave spirit, at an early age he excelled in archery and wrestling. He afterwards applied himself to navigation, in which he acquired considerable fame, and was made capudan of a privateer.   On one occasion, as he was oiling his vessel, Oghlan, an infidel captain, fell upon him, and carried him prisoner to Genoa. On this account Khair-ad-din Pasha sailed against the Genoese with a fleet, threatening that if they did not give up Torghudjeh he would spoil all their villages : whereupon they immediately released him.   The pasha also in a divan spoke so highly of him, saying, Torghudjeh was braver than himself, that they gave him a galley.   After this he was in numerous engagements with Khair-ad-din Pasha in the south, by which he became rich, and increased the number of his ships to twenty-five, with which he began to cruise about.   Having obtained information of the position of Senan Pasha, who was then at sea, he came out to meet him from the south.   On their approach they saluted each other ; but the salute from Torghudjeh's ships being much louder than that of Senan Pasha, the latter suspected him ; and artfully representing to the Porte that his not joining him was a proof of disaffection, and that to subdue him would be a difficult matter, recommended that he should be called to the capital.   Thither Torghudjeh immediately proceeded with eight vessels, and made offers of submission.   With him also came his brave companions in arms, Ghazi Mustaffa, Oluj Ali, Hassan Keleh. Mohammed Reis, Sanjakdar Reis, Deli Jafar, and Kara Kazi, to each of whom a fanar,* and a stipend of seventy or eighty aspres were allotted.   Both before and after his journey to the Sublime Porte, Torghudjeh was engaged in several memorable battles ; a few of which we shall mention.

THE OCCURRENCE AT JARBA.

Whilst Torghudjeh was a capudan of the volunteers, he was on one occasion lying in a harbour called Kantar, in the island of Jarba, where he intended to oil his ships, amounting to eighteen, when Jeghaleh, a Venetian commander, came down upon him with a hundred and fifty vessels, blocked up the entrance to the harbour, threw overboard their ballast, and sat down to enjoy themselves ; conceiving, that when Torghudjeh had exhausted his stock of provisions, they could take him and his ships without any effort.   They even wrote to Genoa, saying they had secured the pirate Torghudjeh and his ships ; and several of their gentlemen fitted out a vessel, and with the intention of taking a voyage of pleasure, sailed towards Jarba.   Torghudjeh, on his part, trusted in God, by whose providence there was in the neighbourhood a small river, navigable by boats, which

* Fanar, a small vessel.

emptied itself into the sea. He therefore set his men to work, and cut a canal two miles in length, by which he conveyed his vessels to sea. He left a tent which he had pitched on the shore, and the infidels supposed he was safe in it. He then proceeded to a place about sixty miles distant, where he completed the oiling of his vessels, and again put out to sea. On his way he met the gentlemen on their voyage of pleasure, and took them prisoners. When the infidels found out that Torghudjeh had made his escape, thinking he had carried his ships overland, they were confounded, and declared that he must be a magician.

CAPTURE OF INFIDEL VESSELS.

Torghudjeh now became the drawn sword of Islamism, and a brave and famous corsair. He frequently attacked the infidels' ships, and destroyed their barges. He once met, at Mania, two barges, laden with corn from Salonica, bound to Venice, which he seized, showing no quarter to those on board. But his feats of this sort are numerous.

THE VISIT OF TORGHUDJEH TO MOGHREB, AND THE INVITATION TO HIM FROM THE EMPEROR.

On one occasion, when this chief was beg of Carli-Eili (Acarnania), he met a Venetian barge, the captain of which, not supposing Torghudjeh to be the principal capudan, and desirous of availing himself as much as possible of the wind, which was then in his favour, neglected to lower his sails, (a mark of respect always shown to great capudans,) or offer any presents. At this, Torghudjeh Beg took umbrage, and began to fire upon the barge from the three ships that were with him. The wind having fallen, she was soon taken; but the capudan having lost one of his brave companions in the conflict, put every one of the infidels to the sword, and burnt the barge. The Venetian ambassador at the Porte, on hearing of this circumstance, went to Rustam Pasha, and lodged a complaint against Torghudjeh. Rustam Pasha, considering Torghudjeh as the enemy of his brother, bore him great hatred, and obtained permission to send a chiaoush to have him summoned to the Porte. Torghudjeh, however, aware of his purpose, sailed with all his vessels to Moghreb, where he remained two years an outlaw. When the capture of Western Trabalos became necessary, the late Sultan Soleiman Khan, whom he had offended, from motives of policy promised him safety, and sent him a copy of the holy book (the Koran) and a golden sword, with a promise that if he should succeed in reducing Trabalos, he should enjoy the begler-begship of that place during his life. The Capudan Senan Pasha was sent with a fleet, and by the direction of Torghudjeh, Trabalos was taken; but its government was given to Senan Pasha; which offended Torghudjeh, who immediately weighed anchor, and directed his course towards Moghreb. He was followed by all the capudans, whose orders were to obey his commands. Senan Pasha being thus left alone, Torghudjeh directed them to return, and some of them with great difficulty reached the Porte.

THE EXPEDITION OF TORGHUDJEH TO BASTIA.

In some historical works it is recorded that, in A. H. 960, Torghudjeh took the command of one hundred and twenty galleys, and sailed to Novocacia. Afterwards, in the month of Rajab, 961, he sailed up the gulf, and besieged Bastia, a Spanish castle on the Italian coast. After many attempts, he was on the point of taking it, when four thousand horse and three thousand infantry came to the assistance of the besieged, and repulsed the Moslems several times. At length, by the favour of God, on the seventh of Ramazan, the abject wretches outside the walls were defeated, and the infidels inside were obliged to fly and abandon the castle. The Moslems allowed forty or fifty of the principal inhabitants their liberty, but put all the others into chains. With the wealth which they found in the castle, and about seven thousand prisoners, they then sailed to Avlona, in the neighbourhood of which the Albanian rebels, by the aid of the governor Ahmed Beg, were vanquished both by sea and land, and rewarded according to their demerits. The Moslems now returned to the Porte with riches far exceeding what they had anticipated. The emperor, who duly appreciated merit, offered Torghudjeh, in addition to his office of capudan, the begler-begship of Algiers. Rustam Pasha, however, prevented his obtaining the latter post, insinuating that Torghudjeh having acquired wealth abroad, had no wish to be employed in the service of the Sublime Porte; and in consequence the sanjak of Carli-Eili (Acarnania) was given to him; but this he declined to accept. The emperor then determined to go out against him, and had actually taken horse for that purpose, when Torghudjeh came out to meet his sovereign, and in person petitioned for the governorship of Trabalos. This was granted him, and he immediately proceeded to Trabalos west, and held his office till he was slain at Malta.

Illustrations of Events, People,
Places, and Ships
Mentioned in the Text of
Tuhfet ül-Kibar fi Esfar il-Bihar

Kemal Reis in battle with Venetians (1499).

The Siege of Rhodes.

Barbarossa Hayreddin.

The Battle of Preveza: Barbarossa's and the Ottoman Empire's greatest naval victory.

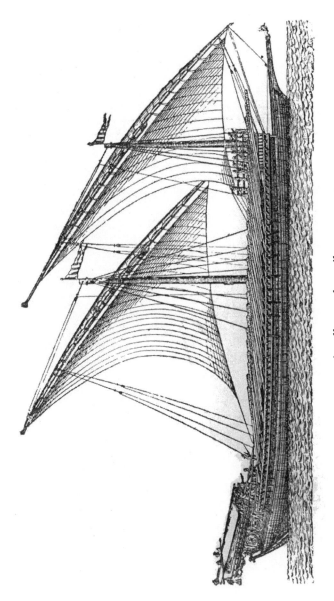

A galley under sail.

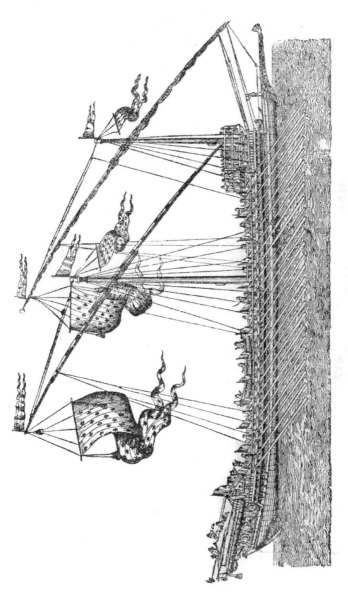

A galley propelled by oars.

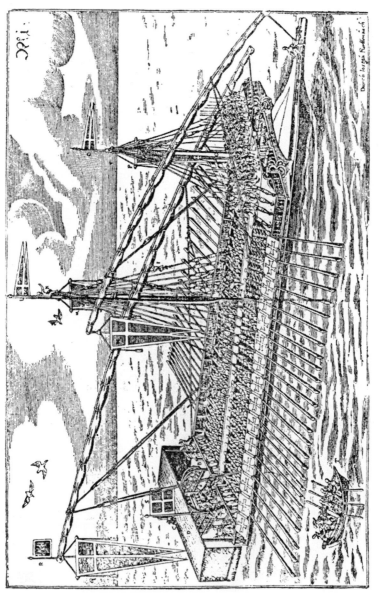

Christian admiral's galley (*reale*).

Andrea Doria, Barbarossa's and Turgut's archenemy.

The fortress of Djerba.

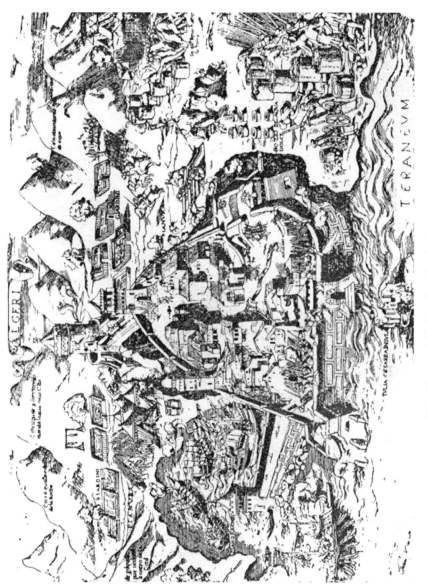

The Siege of Algiers by Charles V in 1541.

Monks ransoming Christian captives in Algiers.

SUPPLEMENTARY
MATERIAL

Summary of Part I,
Chapters 5 through 9, of *Kısm-ı Evvel,*
the First (Narrative) Part

Chapter 5 covers the campaigns of the imperial fleet under the command of Admiral Piyale Pasha—campaigns that spanned a period of 13 years, from 1555 to 1568. Between 1555 and 1558, they consisted chiefly of what we might call today "demonstration cruises" along the coasts and islands belonging to or in league with the Habsburg monarchs of Spain, Charles V and Philip II, and the related cruises designed to assist the king of France, Henri II, Süleyman the Magnificent's ally against their common Habsburg enemy. In 1559, there was the strategically significant cruise to Valona, the Ottoman naval base on the Albanian coast, with the purpose of intervening if the enemy's reported plan to attempt a conquest of Tripoli took place. It did not, and Piyale Pasha sailed back to Istanbul, but the event occurred a year later, and Kâtip Çelebi narrates here the most dramatic and victorious seaborne and amphibious campaign in Ottoman history, the Battle of Djerba in 1560 (remembered in Turkish annals as "Cerbe Vakası"). There followed the failed 1565 campaign to conquer Malta, compensated by the 1566 conquest of Chios. After this success, Piyale Pasha left the post of *kapudan pasha,* or grand admiral, to enter the inner circle of the Ottoman elite as a *kubbe veziri.* The final segment of this chapter relates the consolidation of the Ottoman hold on the important waterways of Mesopotamia, especially the upper Euphrates in present-day Turkey and Syria and both the Euphrates and Tigris through Iraq, in particular their lower course all the way to the Persian Gulf.

Chapter 6 opens with the memorable attempt to dig a canal between the Don and Volga Rivers in 1569; proceeds to the conquest of Cyprus in 1570–1571 followed by the calamitous battle of Lepanto a few weeks later; and winds up with the amazing reconquest of Tunis in 1574 that confounded the portents of Lepanto and confuses modern historians. The chronological span of this chapter, pregnant as it is with events, is thus a mere five years, 1569 to 1574.

Chapter 7 covers the considerably longer period from 1581 to 1643. It relates a gradual retreat of the imperial fleet, which after the recovery of Tunis withdrew from the major combat zone, the central and western Mediterranean. The withdrawal by no means meant an end to the Turkish presence in those waters, for the regencies of Algiers, Tunis, and Tripoli were firmly established and lasted until the nineteenth- and early twentieth- century colonial conquests by France and Italy. The regencies were semi-independent, however, and Kâtip Çelebi restricts his focus to the campaigns of the imperial fleet and its squadrons. This chapter also contains an unexpected novelty: raids made by Cossack seafaring marauders on the Black Sea between 1614 and 1640, and the ultimately successful efforts of the imperial fleet's squadrons to suppress them.

Chapters 8 and 9, the final ones of the *Tuhfet*'s first, narrative part, deal chiefly with the Cretan war. Chapter 8 covers both the war's opening year, 1645, in which the island's second major city and port, Hanya, was conquered, and the return to Istanbul of the expedition's commander, Admiral Yusuf Pasha, greeted as "*Hanya fatihi*" ("conqueror of Hanya"). Chapter 9 recounts the anticlimax to the campaign's successful beginning: the capital of Venetian Crete, Candia, withstood all Turkish assaults, and the republic's fleet not only blockaded the Dardanelles but even, in 1656, defeated that of the Ottoman Empire in a battle which the chronicler Naima described as "the worst naval defeat people of Islam have suffered since the battle of Lepanto" (*Tarih-i Naima*, vol. 6, p. 182). Kâtip Çelebi died, as we have seen, one year after this event, just as the tide was at last turning in the Turks' favor.

The **First Part** ends with a *Tetimme* ("Conclusion"), which is a brief geographical and historical essay on Crete. Kâtip Çelebi mentions as his sources Greek and Latin ones for the pre-Islamic period and Arab ones for the Islamic period. The island had passed through a period of Muslim rule in Abbasid times, and according to the author, it was through trickery that the Byzantine emperor managed to regain it. The essay ends with a *kıssadan hisse*, a "lesson to be learnt from [this] story": "The moral of the story is that it should never be permissible for the rulers of an [Islamic] state, by letting down their guard before an enemy, to display negligence and laziness in the matter of the Holy War on the premise that 'there is no need for it.' Belated regret is useless, what is needed is to be watchful and to solidly protect [the state]." This conclusion comes somewhat as a surprise, for the current campaign aimed at a change of ownership from Christian to Muslim. It may be indicative, however, of the deep-rooted reluctance of a Muslim to accept the passage of a territory that had once been part of the *Dar al-Islam*, "Lands where Islam [rules]," to infidel rule. Crete had once been Islamic, and its fall to the enemy, however remote, should serve as a lesson and, perhaps, as encouragement for a successful conclusion of the ongoing reconquest. Kâtip Çelebi, a pious Muslim and a loyal subject of the Ottoman sultan, wished to contribute by giving useful advice.

Summary of Part II,
Chapters 1 through 7, of *Kısm-ı Sani*,
the Second (Topical) Part

Chapter 1 lists chief admirals (*kapudanan*)[3] of the imperial fleet from what the author states was their beginnings to his own time: 57 individuals, from Baltaoğlu Süleyman Bey, appointed in 1451, to Topal Mehmet Pasha, whose dismissal on 20 December 1657 occurred only after the author's death. The list is on pp. 138-45 of the 1913 Istanbul edition.

Chapter 2 is entitled "The rest of the staff of the arsenal and the military who pertain to the Admiralty. They are of two kinds."

The first kind consists of the staff at the arsenal, whom the author introduces with two appellations: *azeban*, a word of Arabic origin meaning "bachelor,"[4] and the less intriguing "*tersane halkı*," the arsenal employees. These include naval officers, whom he calls *kapudanlar* and *reisler* (*kapudan* is of Italian origin, *reis* of Arabic origin; both mean "captain," with the nuance that *kapudan* refers to a higher rank, starting with *kapudan paşa* or *kaptanpaşa*, the admiral); technical staff such as caulkers (*kalafatçılar*); bombardiers (*kumbaracılar*); carpenters (*neccarlar*); and so forth: 1,893 individuals in all.

The second kind consists of those governors (*beys*) of the empire's coastal or insular districts (*sancaks*) who were expected to join with their ships the imperial fleet on its campaigns. The chapter discusses primarily the organizational and financial structure of this system.

Chapter 3 takes as its subject the rules (*kanun*) and procedures regulating the expeditions of the imperial fleet.

"The ships leave from Beşiktaş, and when they arrive at Yedikule, they stay there one or two days for troops to come aboard. From there they proceed to Ereğli, and, exiting from the Marmara Sea, they come to Ekinlik, Galipoli, and, on the outer side of Boğaz Hisarı, to Piyale Pasa Bahcesi Selvilikleri [or Cypress Groves of Piyale Pasha's garden]. These places, separated from one another by some fifty to sixty miles, are anchorages; the ships stop at each of these harbors safe from surprise attack. The fleet stays at Cypress Groves one day, getting a fresh supply of water, and sending *sandals* (rowboats)[5] to the Boğaz-Hisar on the opposite side, each to bring 30 logs of chip pine wood for tallowing[6] the ships, because it is unavailable anywhere else. When they arrive in this harbor, two good galiots set out on a scouting mission, anchoring two to three miles ahead of the fleet, because the security the fleet had enjoyed before leaving the Straits no longer exists outside. The fleet then proceeds in this manner every time it stops at a harbor. After morning prayer, they set out: like a brood-hen with chicks under her wings, the *baştarda* in the middle, the other ships around it, they advance at a leisurely pace—they do not hurry like a dispatch boat. If the aforementioned scout galiots, three miles ahead, see something unusual, they alert [the fleet's commanders]. The arsenal warden (*tersane kahyasî*), with ten good galleys, guards the fleet's rear: at night he lights a lamp (*fener*), and takes in tow ships that have problems, such as those whose sails were torn or yards broken in a storm—this is the rescue squadron that sails behind the fleet. Moreover, two *bey* ships sail one hour after the fleet so that, if there are any scattered troops left behind, they may collect them.

"From Baba burnu (Cape Baba) the fleet proceeds to Sivrice harbor, Lesbos (Midilli) and Chios (Sakız), and from there it turns toward the coast of Rum Ili: to Euboea (Ağriboz), Methoni (Modon), and Navarino (Anavarin). The last-named harbor is an assemblage point, both a terminus of the Ottoman fleet's home range as well as its advanced base facing the infidels to the west of there. Two good galiots are sent to the infidels' side to capture persons for intelligence purposes. Five hundred miles from Navarino on the opposite side, Messina has the comparable function as the assemblage point and advanced base of the infidel fleet. Ships of the Pope, Malta, the Duke [of Florence], and Spain come there and exchange information with Venice.

"Ships do not spend the night on the open sea—this is not a regulation but a precautionary measure. The distance from Rhodes to Alexandria, however, is 500 miles; with favorable winds it can be crossed while spending two nights at large, otherwise the voyage can include three to four nights. From Methoni and Navarino the distance to Tripoli is 700 miles; a voyage with favorable winds will include three nights at large, otherwise, [even] with the help of oars, the crossing will take five to six days. In such situations, it is advised that if a storm breaks out, each ship should light a lantern; even those that do not have an [official] lantern should do so, lest they collide with one another in the storm. And [the navigators of] each ship, measuring its progress day and night with dead reckoning (*kiyas*), check it on the map (*harti*), and if contrary wind has turned it in the wrong direction, they make a pencil mark on the map and correct the course.

"During a campaign (*sefer*), a ship is tallowed two to three times. The first tallowing takes place at Navarino, where the ships have arrived after a cruise via Chios to Euboea and Methoni on the Rumelian coast. One more tallowing takes place at Foça on the Anatolian coast. First to be tallowed are the ships of the imperial fleet, while those of the governors stand guard outside; once that is done, the latter too are tallowed. It is forbidden to tallow them all at the same time, a rule established at a specific date by Halil Pasha.

"A well-tallowed ship travels twice as fast as one that has not been tallowed—for example, while a ship that had not been tallowed for a long time covers, in a favorable wind, a distance of ten miles in an hour, a newly tallowed one covers twenty miles."

Chapter 4 is entitled "On the Manner in which a Sea Battle is Fought according to regulations."

"First of all, when our fleet encounters that of the infidels along the Anatolian or Rumelian coast, the procedure it adopts should be the following: If our fleet is inshore and the infidel one is farther out, a confrontation should be avoided, because it would bring trouble—soldiers on board would pay attention only to the shore: a sea battle is deadly business, beyond the grasp of those who have never been in one. In a situation of this type, everyone tries to make it to the shore. If, however, it is the infidel fleet that is near the coast and ours outside, or if the coast is that of infidel territory, or if both fleets are on the high seas, in each of these three cases the Turks can deliver battle to the infidel: for the ship is the only place of survival, so that the soldiers will fight.

"Thus far we have discussed battles in the Mediterranean. As for regulations pertaining to combating Cossacks[7] on the Black Sea, their *shaykas*[8] set out from the Dnepr (Özü) to raid the coasts of that region. If they happen to be some fifteen miles or even more out in the open sea, galleys attack them without any fear, and in favorable wind they crush them—a hundred *shaykas* cannot withstand one galley, as the battle fought by Recep Pasha illustrates. If, however, [the *shaykas*] are near the shore, [the galleys] do not go after them there; they would run aground and bring shame on our side, as happened on the campaign led by Cigalazade Mahmut Pasha."[9]

Chapter 5 discusses the types of ships in the imperial navy and their crews.

Wars in the Mediterranean were fought since antiquity primarily with oar-propelled ships, of which the best-known type and name is the galley, *kadırga* in Turkish. By Kâtip Çelebi's time, however, warships propelled exclusively by wind-and-sail power, then known in Turkish by the generic term *kalyon* (derived from *galleon*, which, however, in Western languages has a more specific connotation) had begun to oust the galleys from their dominant position, but not yet in the Ottoman Empire. Our author thus devotes the greater part of this chapter to the oar-propelled category, *çektiri*, or *çektirir*, in Turkish. The classifications of ships within this category are based on the number of thwarts or oar benches per ship. He lists the following types:

Fırkata, 10 to 17 oar benches; each oar is pulled by two
     to three men.

Perkende, 18 to 19 oar benches.

Kalita, 19 to 24 oar benches.

Kadırga, 25 oar benches; each oar is pulled by four men.

Baştarda, 26 to 36 oar benches; each oar is pulled by five
     to seven men.

Mavna: "According to some, if a [*baştarda*] is still higher and
     wider, it is a *mavna.*"

Kâtip Çelebi dispenses with the *kalyon* category, pure sailing ships,
with the following brief paragraph: "The galleon category too consists
of several types, but since they are not used in our navy except the
burton—and it too has only recently come into use—we shall not go
into further details. It is mostly the infidels who use them. There are
several kinds, from polikatas to caracks, which are Spain's warships.
We shall discuss our own ships." The author then discusses in greater
detail the *kadırga, baştarda,* and *mavna,* their crews and equipment.
There is a certain degree of inconsistency and contradiction in his
text, no doubt prompted by the complexity of an intrinsically difficult
subject to which he, a landlubber-and-library scholar, was a stranger,
and he may have forgotten or misunderstood certain data. By and
large, however, his description is clear enough to allow us to translate
the terms he uses for the three ships as ordinary galley, the admiral's
galley, and galeass.

Chapter 6 describes the kinds and quantity of material needed for
building and maintaining a fleet, and the approximate amount the
treasury spends on it.

Chapter 7, the final one, entitled "Advice by Corsairs on the Matter
of the Sea and the Fleet," is as original as it is characteristic of the Ottoman conception of sea power. The author prefaces this chapter
with a forceful reminder that the greatness of the "august state"

(*devlet-i aliye*), the Ottoman Empire, to a considerable degree hinges on "*umur-i derya*," maritime and naval matters; for "besides the fact that the empire's splendor and renown derives from extending its command over two continents and two seas (*revnak ve unvanı berreyn ve bahreyne hükümle olduğundan gayrı*), whose provinces and islands are lined by sea coasts (*sevahil-i derya*), the abode of the sublime sultanate, Istanbul (*dar es-saltanat-i aliye yani Kustantiniye*), is felicitously located by two seas. Moreover, Muslims passed into Europe, the foremost of the four segments of the world, only recently. In Rumelia, their sovereigns conquered parts of Bosnia and Hungary; these are Europe's borderland, and since their acquisition, conservation, and protection have been based on the control of the sea (*derya elde olmağla mevkuf olduğundan*), they attached great importance to this fact. It is so still now, and the current negligence should be abandoned (*olan gafleti koyup*) and replaced by a determined effort (*bezl-i makdûr*) [to set things right again]. May God the Sublime grant [us] success (*Allah teâlâ muvaffak eyliye*)!"

After this prologue, the author proceeds to offer forty different kinds of advice:

"ADVICE NO. 1: The admiral, if he himself is not a corsair (*korsan*),[10] in naval matters and war at sea should consult with corsairs and listen to them. He should avoid relying on his own judgment alone; those who did so have usually come to regret it. Moreover, if a mistake is made in these matters, this should also save him from being the only one to bear the blame.

ADVICE NO. 2: Ships for the fleet should be built, as much as possible, at the imperial navy yard (*tersane-i amire*). This process is faster, and the vessels are delivered on time. Moreover, it lightens the burden (*zulüm*, lit. violence) imposed on the people.

ADVICE NO. 3: Effort should be made to prevent the equipment of ships from becoming incomplete. Every aspect should be taken care of on time; negligence should not be tolerated.

ADVICE NO. 4: When the fleet has left the Straits, patrolling missions should not be neglected. While the fleet is under way, two good galiots should sail two miles ahead, and when it lies in a harbor, they should anchor two to three miles offshore. Two ships of the *beys* should follow the fleet at a distance of one hour's sailing, in order to gather wayward soldiers.

ADVICE NO. 5: If the fleet is 200 ships strong, it should split up into two groups. 100 units should sail, with the Pasha of Rhodes, one day before [the other], because not every harbor can accommodate the whole fleet. They used to proceed like this in the past, but there were few harbors capable of that. In the case of islands, ships may anchor on any side of them, provided that it is the lee side, opposite to the direction of the wind. The mainland coast, however, does not offer such alternatives.

ADVICE NO. 6: If a fleet arrives at a harbor in the afternoon—whether it is in the midst of the [Aegean] archipelago or on the Anatolian or Rumelian side—it should stay there instead of spurning it on the premise that 'there is another harbor [down the road],' because [to reach it on the same day] the likelihood is slim: weather can become windy, and the fleet becomes scattered by staying out at night. It is a mistake to lie [outside an anchorage] except on the high seas [where there is no other choice].

ADVICE NO. 7: Once the Straits have been left behind, a fleet should not set out without performing the morning prayer.

ADVICE NO. 8: *Baştarda* captains ought to be men who for years had practiced the trade of *course* (*korsanlık*) at Algiers and elsewhere, because the fleet's efficient operations, whether in action or at rest, depend on their experience.

ADVICE NO. 9: While a fleet is in progress, the rowers of the *baştarda* should move [the oars] like an eagle flaps its wings, slowly, they should avoid haste similar to that of rapid dispatch boats [*ulak*], [despite the] well-known criticism of Spanish captains who taunt [the Turks] saying 'your ships are not fast.' On this side [of the argument], expert corsairs retort, 'Our ships do not chase those who flee, and do not flee from those who chase.'[11]

ADVICE NO. 10: *Bey* ships should always precede the *baştarda*. The contents of its hold should not depend on the desire to increase its speed. A *baştarda* does not have to be fast, and must not pass the *bey* ships; should that happen, it would be like giving the galley slaves (prisoner rowers, *forsalar*) permission to seize the ship.

ADVICE NO. 11: When ships are tallowed, the fleet should form two groups: while one is worked on, the other stands guard before taking its turn. Much harm has often been incurred when the enemy surprised a fleet all of whose units were being tallowed at the same time.

ADVICE NO. 12: When the fleet arrives at Navarino, two good galiots should be sent to the infidels' side with the mission of seizing persons for intelligence interrogation. If [it turns out that] an infidel fleet is being assembled at Messina, [the Turkish] fleet should guard [Ottoman] coasts instead of undertaking any sailing elsewhere.

ADVICE NO. 13: If there is no infidel fleet at Messina, and the captains wish to go to the infidels' shores or undertake a cruise on the high seas, at Navarino they should prepare (*bozalar*, lit. deconstruct) fifteen ships, which means that they replace the weak ones among the crews with a selection of strong and able rowers and marines.

ADVICE NO. 14: If it is necessary to undertake a cruise from Navarino, water barrels should be filled with a fifteen day[s'] supply. The fleet having left the harbor after the evening prayer, the *reaya*[12] of Navarino should not fail to light a fire on a high place for the duration of one day and one night, so that, if a storm breaks out and the fleet has to return, it can find the way back to port. Placing a specific person over them [for the supervision of this task] might be a good idea.

ADVICE NO. 15: If a cruise on the high seas is planned, the crews should be admonished that, should a storm break out at night, a lantern be lit on each ship. On those that do not have [fixed] lanterns they should hang one, to avoid the danger of ships colliding with one another.

ADVICE NO. 16: The [Aegean] Archipelago abounds in shoals and eddies, thirty different kinds of [strong] winds, [capable of making a ship] fail to reach its destination. Each island is marked by a different vortex, and there are also plenty of reefs—situations in which many a ship has met its doom; [mariners] call the Archipelago 'the fleets' graveyard' [*kınnare*, lit. slaughterhouse].

ADVICE NO. 17: When the fleet sails along the coasts of Rumelia or Anatolia, ten galiots should perform guard duty in the Archipelago. This was what the Admirals in the past used to do.

ADVICE NO. 18: If a fleet runs into a fog during a cruise: Near the coast, ships should without delay drop anchor and not move until the fog has cleared. On the high seas, the band on the admiral's *baştarda* should start playing, and those on the other ships should do likewise, not stopping until the fog has cleared, to prevent the fleet's dispersal.

ADVICE NO. 19: Captains (*reisler*) should strive to gain expertise in the maritime profession (*derya ilmi*, lit. sea science). They should not neglect checking the compass and the chart (*pusula ve harti*), and treat those expert in this matter with great courtesy. [Captains] lacking such expertise should make efforts to acquire it.

ADVICE NO. 20: The admiral (*kapudan paşa*) should subject [the captains] to examination[s], as Derviş Pasha used to do. Derviş Pasha, making the salaries contingent on [the captains' expertise with] the compass and the chart, appointed an expert individual named Misli Çavuş examiner on this matter, while the other sailors (*gemiciler*) were examined on such matters as how to tie a hawser (*palamar bağlamak*). Salaries were given [according to the results], at which point the ignorant ones became eager to learn.

ADVICE NO. 21: If the fleet encounters that of the infidels, and it happens in a situation where ours is near the Rumelian or Anatolian shore while that of the infidels is at large, a clash with the latter should be avoided, [the commanders] pretending not to have noticed it. If, however, our ships are at large and those of the infidels near the shore, or if the shore is that of infidel territory, or if both have met on the high seas, in each of these three situations it is all right to attack the infidel. We have explained the reasons for this procedure in the chapter on war [i.e, chapter 4].

ADVICE NO. 22: If the enemy is a galleon (*kalyon*), immediate attack should be avoided; rather, the ship should be subjected to prolonged bombardment from a distance, to inflict damage such as a broken rudder and mast, and only then [the galleon] should be approached. And if there is [too much] wind, they take up the chase [of the enemy ships], in the open sea, with the *borda*-sail[13] set, and bombarding them they go on until there is a lull.

ADVICE NO. 23: In a battle, galleys should form an orderly line (*saf saf dizile*). The admiral's ship should stay in the rear, accompanied by five ships: three behind, two in front.

ADVICE NO. 24: The grand admiral, as the commander, should stay on his ship and not leave it under any pretext; instead, he should send his officers (*ağas*) to lead the soldiers. In such situations it is against the regulations and dangerous for the top commander to move around in a boat (*kayık*).

ADVICE NO. 25: The grand admiral should stay at his command post and not try to attack the enemy himself. 'When the head is gone, the feet do not remain stable.' Much harm has been incurred because of [the infraction] of this [rule]. The top commander functions best if he stays at his command post.

ADVICE NO. 26: The *beys* should remove from each of their many ships one hundred infidels and replace them with Turks; those who do not comply should be called to order —many a *bey* ship has been lost when galley slaves (*forsas*) seized it.

ADVICE NO. 27: The oarsmen should be *muşakkar*, which means a mix of Turks and *forsas*. In the past, admirals picked their choice of the best oarsmen, three *forsas* and three Turks [per thwart] for their *baş-tardas*. One ought to be wary of *forsas*, and avoid manning the ships of the Istanbul [arsenal] with [too] many [foreign] infidels; rather the officially registered government infidels (*miri kafir*)[15] should be distributed among the ships. Captains should not consent to place fifty infidels in a ship; it is better, as far as possible, if the Turks are the oarsmen instead of coveting the *forsas*' proficiency— countless ships have been lost by being seized by them.

ADVICE NO. 28: When a fleet sails out, [the commanders] should make sure to send a good galiot with the purpose of seizing persons for intelligence gathering. In the past they used to send [ships] with this mission to the infidel side, but now that is no longer necessary; [such persons] should come from the [Aegean] archipelago.

ADVICE NO. 29: When in a battle some of a ship's crew are hit by cannon or falconet (*zarbzen*) fire, the dead and wounded should be instantly taken to the hold and covered. Showing them to the crew causes disarray, confusion and fear.

ADVICE NO. 30: If [Turks] manage to seize a ship [in a battle], they should first examine its guns and, if need be, spike them. Booty should not preoccupy them before the battle has been won and [the enemy] curbed.

ADVICE NO. 31: If in a battle a ship is hit by cannon fire below the waterline, and it turns out to be impossible to quickly close [the hole], a long piece of cloth like a turban or a towel should be placed there so as to make it absorb the water flow and plug the spot. Some ships have been saved in this manner from foundering.

ADVICE NO. 32: Gunners should be expert in their trade, and should train novices. On a ship each gun should be handled by a master gunner.

ADVICE NO. 33: Gunpowder must be glazed (*perdaht*). Way back in Salih Pasha's time procurement of gunpowder was ordered from Egypt, since glazing is best done there, so that most of this material comes from that country.

While the infidels' guns have a 12-span caliber, the thrust of the gunpowder used by them makes the range of their guns considerably exceed that of our 16-span guns.[15]

ADVICE NO. 34: Due importance should be attached to mortar shells as well as to arrows and [other] tools for burning the sails of enemy ships. Tools for defense should not be neglected [either].

ADVICE NO. 35: Since of old [regular] troops have been the ones who carried out conquests on land, there should be no desire to sign up *levents*.[16] Rather, [regular] troops should be used, according to specific situations.

ADVICE NO. 36: After a galleon has assisted the departure of the fleet from the Straits, it should return instead of accompanying it. [The galleon] would tie it down, bringing no benefit, and perhaps even do harm.

ADVICE NO. 37: A fleet should be unencumbered and nimble at sea, able to proceed in any direction. This is what makes it defeat the infidels, because their oarships, [even if] separated from galleons, cannot keep up with our fleet. As for the movement of a galleon, it depends on the wind.

ADVICE NO. 38: Importance should be attached to the conquest (*garet*, lit. raid) of the island of Corfu and to the construction of fortresses on the shore. This is the way to breach the defenses (*erkân*, lit. pillars) of the infidels.

ADVICE NO. 39: The conquest of the fortresses of Corfu and Zadar is not considered to be easy. If such a project is undertaken, it should start with careful planning and preparations, an effort equal to that made by Sultan Bayezid for the conquest of the fortress of Lepanto.

ADVICE NO. 40: Now that we have presented the epic of the campaigns and conquests of past [Ottoman] sovereigns, and of the sailings and battles waged by the imperial fleet, may a lesson be drawn from it, and not be left unheeded. Greetings."

The book ends with a brief chapter whose title is "Hatimetü'l-Kitap ve Fezleketü'l-Hesap" ("Epilogue of the Book and Summary of the Account"). It consists of two parts, of which the first contains reflections on man as part of God's creation, and his duty to accept God's decrees whatever they are. The second part, however, takes an important step beyond that somewhat fatalistic attitude. Kâtip Çelebi discusses here the causes of the troubling state of the Ottoman Empire:

"At present, . . . if a way is sought to find remedies to the insolence (*tuğyan*) of the enemies, to the lack of means, soldiers, and money, and to the riotousness of the subjects, it is by returning to the laws (*kanun*) laid by the elders, by reactivating them and respecting them. The sovereigns who conquered and subdued the well-protected lands by the sword as well as through wise measures, especially Sultan Selim the First and Sultan Süleyman Khan (together with the 'scholar of Rum' Kemal Paşazade Efendi and Ebu's-Suud Efendi), paid great attention to applying those laws on the basis of the holy law (*şer'-i şerif*), while [also] endeavoring to complete what was missing in them. This august empire found its stability thanks to the effects of those blessed efforts, and whatever adversity there appeared did it little damage. Those who came after them, however, deemed whatever they did to be law: new laws were established, and it was forgotten to act the right way. From now on, recovery of what has been lost, and removal of the deficiencies, should be based on applying to the utmost degree possible the old law (*kanun-i kadim*). The Sovereign who is the refuge of the world—may God give him a long life—and who knows these laws, should start by reactivating every one of them, with the sword of the holy law (*seyf-i şerif*) and the law of policy (*kanun-i siyaset*): that is the absolute condition. May God the Sublime make it possible! Amen."

The Battle of Djerba (1560)[17]: Kâtip Çelebi's Sources and His Account

Comments on the Excerpt
"The Djerba Campaign" ("*Sefer-i Cerbe*")

The phenomenal exploits of Hayreddin Barbarossa, first as a free-lance *gazi*-corsair, then as *beylerbeyi*, or governor of Algiers, and finally as admiral of the sultan's navy, gave rise to the image of the Ottoman Empire as the foremost naval power of the time. It was Hayreddin's victory in the battle of Prevesa (1538), however, that sealed the reputation of the Turks as invincible at sea. Thus when in 1541 Emperor Charles V, Sultan Süleyman the Magnificent's rival for what some view as a contest for world dominance, decided to conquer Algiers, the center of Ottoman power in the Western Mediterranean, he set out with the huge armada only in October. He did so on the premise that worsening weather conditions would prevent Hayreddin and the imperial fleet from coming to the province's rescue all the way from Istanbul. He was proven right, but autumn storms and heavy rainfall did not spare the Christians either, and helped the *beylerbey* Hasan Pasha defeat Charles, who sailed back discouraged and humiliated.

Hayreddin died in 1546, but the aura spread by him endured. Turgut Reis was his most valiant disciple, and in 1551 he assisted Admiral Sinan Pasha in the conquest of Tripoli from the Knights of St. John established on Malta. He was then appointed the port city's and the province's *beylerbeyi*, and Tripoli became, after Algiers, another thorn in the flank of Christian, especially Habsburg, shipping and coasts. Charles V and then his son Philip II felt obliged to endure the always present Turkish threat partly because their ever-resuming wars with the kings of France consumed nearly the totality of their resources.

The French burden was finally lifted on 3 April 1559 with the peace treaty of Cateau-Cambrésis. Philip II did not need much persuasion when Jean Parisot de la Valette, grand master of the order at Malta, turned to him with a request that an expedition be undertaken to recover Tripoli from the Turks. The Sublime Porte, perfectly aware of the planned attack, did not remain idle. Piyale Pasha, admiral of the Ottoman navy,[18] was sent with a fleet on a cruise to the strategically located port of Valona in the Adriatic, ready to act if necessary. It was not, because the Christians were not ready, and the delay may have been partly prompted by the idea that it might be best to set out late in the fall season after the return of Piyale Pasha's fleet to Istanbul; if so, it was an ominous repetition of Charles V's 1541 mistake. The Christian fleet assembled at Messina in November and proceeded to the Sicilian port of Syracuse, which it then left on 1 December with Tripoli as its target. Winter storms cut the sailing short, however, and the fleet took refuge at Malta, where it then stayed until on 10 February 1560 it finally set out for Tripoli.

The expedition was under the overall command of Philip II's viceroy of Sicily, Juan de la Cerda, Duke of Medinaceli. Gian-Andrea Doria, grandnephew of the famous Andrea Doria,[19] had the naval command; Don Álvaro de Sande, that of the troops. War galleys and transports, sailing ships called *barça* in Turkish, constituted the fleet. They were a composite lot of squadrons supplied by the viceroyalties of Sicily and Naples, the republic of Genoa, the Papal States, the duchy of Florence, the Knights of Malta, the principality of Monaco, and a few private individuals. Doria, besides holding the overall naval command, led a squadron of seventeen mostly Genoese galleys, one of which was the *reale* (the naval commander's flagship, corresponding to the Turkish *baştarda*), with him on board. Among the other commanders, Don Berenguer de Requesens led the squadron of the viceroyalty of Sicily; Don Sancho de Leyva, that of the viceroyalty of Naples; Charles de Tessières, that of Malta. Altogether there were some fifty war galleys, besides twenty-eight transports under Andrea Gonzaga. When we step back and take a broader view of this armada, we realize that by modern standards it was preponderantly Italian, though with the conspicuous absence of Venice. The Italian nature of the naval part is further emphasized by the absence of the Spanish fleet; Philip II had indeed ordered his admiral, Juan de Mendoza, to stay with Spain's galleys closer to home in order to protect its coasts against Muslim corsairs. The troops on board were chiefly Spanish, Italian, and German. Their number was some ten thousand men. It would have been larger and in better shape if the expedition had not been forced to spend the winter in Malta, with adverse weather conditions and poor accommodation taking a terrible toll on the participants who for the most part had to stay aboard.

Nevertheless, with good leadership, it might not have been impossible to carry out the mission. The *beylerbeyi* of Tripoli, Turgut Pasha, although himself a great mariner and a brave corsair, had problems with his untrustworthy Arab neighbors such as the shaykh of Qayrawan or, still worse, with those who were not averse to collaborating with the Spaniards, for example, the Hafsid ruler of Tunis. The Ottoman garrison at Tripoli was small—some 500 men[20] —and a sudden landing of the Christians might have swung many of the Arabs to their side. The two top commanders displayed, however, fatal indecisiveness. The Duke of Medinaceli knew nothing about naval matters and was more a politician than a military man. Gian-Andrea Doria, a young man of twenty years, held this post thanks only to his prestigious great-uncle, and lacked both sufficient experience and authority among the other captains. Instead of attacking Tripoli forthwith, Medinaceli and Doria procrastinated along the coast, and finally, as an interim measure, decided to occupy Djerba. They landed troops on 7 March and set about consolidating the already somewhat present Spanish suzerainty, the ruling shaykh swearing on the Qur'an that he would be loyal to the Spanish king. The Christians also proceeded to build a strong fort on the northern coast of the island.

The flaw of swerving from the main purpose of the expedition, elimination of Tripoli as a corsair base and recovering it for the Maltese knights, to the less relevant Djerba, was made worse by a new belief that domestic problems—a struggle between his sons Bayezid and Selim—would prevent Süleyman the Magnificent from dealing effectively with the Christian attack. The Duke of Medinaceli was then disabused by reports from Istanbul that an expedition of the imperial fleet was indeed being prepared, but his calculation that Piyale Pasha would not be able to reach the critical area before June made him tarry with the planned departure, which he did perhaps partly to allow some of his commanders to engage in what might have turned into lucrative commercial ventures, purchasing and loading commodities such as fabrics woven from wool produced on the island, dates, olives, horses, and camels. The greatest flaw, however, was naval: one at the top, for Doria clearly was not up to the challenge; the other at the base: the pervasive conviction that the Turks were invincible at sea, and that under the present circumstances, "a good escape is worth more than a brave battle."[21]

Kâtip Çelebi and his principal source, Zekeriyyazade, give a fairly accurate account, confirmed by Christian sources, of the naval debacle that befell the expedition upon the arrival of Piyale Pasha with his fleet. They attribute Turkish victory to the religiously inspired zeal of the Muslim *gazis*, and to a degree this is undoubtedly true. There were a whole range of additional causes, however. Besides the overwhelming Turkish reputation, one was the exemplary discipline of the Ottoman fleet and competent leadership by Piyale Pasha, ably assisted by the other commanders, in contrast to the incompetence marking his opponents. At Djerba, Gian-Andrea Doria's fleet, instead of fighting, strove to flee. This stands in sharp contrast to the Christian troops besieged on Djerba. Their three months' long resistance was nothing short of heroic.

Neither Turkish author could provide an accurate account of the Christian expedition's leadership. Mentioning the commander of the naval forces, Andrea Doria's grandnephew Gian-Andrea Doria, as the "son of Andrea Doria" is the closest either of them comes to adequate identification. The only other name mentioned is "Donabur," for Don Álvaro de Sande. The Duke of Medinaceli, viceroy of Sicily, is not mentioned by name but only as the "*kapudan* of the island of Ci-cilye,"[22] and Don Sancho de Leyva, commander of the galleys of Naples, is "Anabolu kapudanı" (the governor [*kapudan*] of Anabolu). It could create a misidentification if he is put on a par with Medi-naceli, for the viceroy of Naples was at that time Pedro Afán de Rib-era, Duke of Alcalá, who was absent from Djerba. Kâtip Çelebi does not report that both Doria and Medinaceli slipped out at night early after the beginning of the siege, escaping in fast galleys to Malta and then to their homes in Sicily and Italy.[23] They thereby avoided the or-deal that was in store for the others, with Don Álvaro de Sande at the command. After the triumphal return of Piyale Pasha with the fleet to Istanbul on 27 September 1560, and the presentation of the cap-tured men and booty to the sultan and the divan on 28 September, a public procession of the captives through the streets of the capital took place: three noblemen—Don Álvaro de Sande, Don Berenguer de Requesens, and Don Sancho de Leyva—riding on horseback, the others marching on foot. Once the celebrations were over, the cap-tives were divided into two groups; those likely to produce ransom money were taken to prison, the rest were distributed in the imperial navy as galley slaves. People like Don Berenguer and Don Sancho soon returned home, but not Don Álvaro, for Süleyman apparently vowed that he would never let him go free. In December 1560, how-ever, Charles IX ascended the throne as the new king of France, and Philip II asked his French peer to intervene with France's traditional ally, the Ottoman sultan, to grant the release of the prisoner as a spe-cial favor on *his*, Charles's, enthronement. The sultan did, and the Spanish nobleman returned to his home country.[24]

Like names of individuals, place names may often present a prob-lem for the reader of the Turkish text, although less so for Kâtip Çelebi himself. By "Anabolu kapudanı" he surely meant the captain of the Naples squadron, in other words, Don Sancho de Leyva. How-ever, he uses the same name for the other Naples, "Napoli di Roma-nia" or Nauplio, the fortified harbor fortress on the northeastern coast of the Peloponnese, and only the context can tell us which one is meant.

Kâtip Çelebi's account of this event, in chapter 5 of the first (narrative) part, is on fols. 60a-63b of TSMK Revan ms. 1292, reproduced in the 2008 Ankara facsimile edition; on fols. 33b-35b of the 1729 Müteferrika edition; on pp. 73-78 of the 1913 Istanbul edition; on pp. 108-115 of Orhan Şaik Gökyay's modernized version; and on pp. 100-102 of the 2008 Ankara English translation. Our translation is based both on the 1913 Istanbul edition and on the Ankara facsimile edition.

"The Djerba Campaign" ("*Sefer-i Cerbe*"): Translated Excerpt from the Last Third of the Narrative Part

When the winter season had passed and spring came, on 8 Recep 967 / 4 April 1560 admiral Piyale Pasha sailed out with 120 galleys.[25] As he reached Koyun Island,[27] there came a *firkata* sent by the governor of Tripoli, Turgut Pasha, with the report that the fleet of the abject infidel was in the vicinity of the island of Djerba, preparing to attack Tripoli.

Meanwhile the above-mentioned pasha sent captain (*reis*) Uluç Ali,[27] one of that time's renowned corsairs, with several galleys to infidel quarters in order to seize someone for intelligence interrogation (*dil*, lit. tongue). Uluç Ali ran into an enemy *barça*;[28] while they were engaged in an exchange of gunfire, several more [Turkish] ships reached the scene, and after intense battery they seized the ship, capturing its accursed crew. These prisoners, together with guns and [other] equipment, were sent to the capital (*asitane*, lit. threshold, i.e., Istanbul).

When the fleet reached the roadstead of Modon, the *bey* of Rhodes, Kurtoğlu Ahmet Bey, and that of the *sancak* ("district") of Lesbos, Mustafa Bey, arrived with several ships and joined the fleet amidst great festivities. After resting there several days, during which the ships were tallowed and provisions and equipment were completed, the expedition, placing its trust in God, sailed on the evening of 5 Şaban / 1 May westward in the direction of North Africa (*Mağrib*).

Raiding the Island of Malta

When, after four days and four nights of progress with the aid of a favorable wind, it was ascertained that the fleet had reached the vicinity of the island of Malta, sails were lowered. The next day the fleet approached Little Malta,[29] and a group of warriors went ashore, falling upon the habitations of the infidels. Having gathered much booty, they set fire to their houses, gardens and orchards, and seized persons well suited for interrogation. From them the expedition's leaders learned that 49 galleys and 36 *barças* were now riding at anchor in the shoals of Djerba, unaware of the approach of Muslim ships. A galiot that had previously come from Turgut Pasha was sent back to him at Tripoli with this news, and the imperial fleet, placing its trust in the Lord, set out toward the abject infidel's fleet. After having sailed two days and two nights, it reached the shoals of Kerkenna near Djerba, and dropped anchor. The next day, all the weapons and tools of war were made ready, and the fleet got under way, anchoring within 12 miles of Djerba. The island is situated near the shore 200 miles west of Tripoli.[30] There used to be a causeway linking it to the shore, but the causeway was then cut.

Battle of Piyale Pasha with the Infidel's Fleet

When the imperial fleet had earlier arrived at Malta, the island's infidels sent a boat informing [those at Djerba] about it. The abject infidels weighed anchor and advanced with their ships some seven to eight miles, ready for confrontation. In the morning the soldiers of Islam too, seeing the infidel ships, set out amidst various kinds of trappings and pomp. At first there was some exchange of gunfire, but seeing that the Muslims were on the attack, the infidels decided to flee. One group sought safety beneath the fortress of Djerba, another group sailed out into the open sea. The Pasha too divided his ships into two groups: one was sent after those who had moved to the fortress, while he himself, catching up with those that had sailed out, engaged in battle. Muslim ships accosted the galleys of the abject infidels, and in each fierce fighting took place. In the end the soldiers of Islam prevailed, and the abject infidels were defeated and humiliated. Twenty galleys and 26 *barças* stayed in the shoals, some sunk, some captured, some burned. From among the infidel commanders, the governor (*kapudan*) of Anabolu and his sons, the son of Andrea Doria, and the governor of Sicily, frightened out of their wits, jumped into *firkatas* and retreated into the fortress of the island. In sum, on that day the infidel fleet suffered total destruction—never before had there been a defeat of this magnitude.

The fortress in question had since of old been inhabited by Muslims, but somehow it fell into the hands of the infidels. Its important conquest [was organized in the following manner:] the imperial fleet secured the maritime side, while on land it was the task of the *beylerbeyi* of Tripoli, Turgut Pasha, and of other commanders and their valiant arquebusiers, some mounted, some on foot, from the coastland of Tripoli, Kayrawan, and Sfax. The tight siege, imposed from/on [all] four sides, began on 3 Ramazan / 28 May. When [the Muslims] were about to occupy their parapets (*metris*), the infidels made a night sally, with much arrow and arquebus shooting. The *gazis*, however, charged them with drawn swords, so that the accursed ones lost courage and fled. Many infidels fell on the ground, and the parapets were secured. The infidels dug a second large trench (*hendek*) in front of the one by the fortress, and strung around it a fortified encampment (*etrafina tabur çevirip*)[31] into which three thousand men were placed: there they were staying under awnings and in tents, guarding the site. In one spot there was a well, and since [the infidels] got most of their water supply from it, they constructed strong parapets over it, protecting it with guns manned by 800 men. They drew water for the fortress from it day and night; Muslim soldiers, advancing close to this well, mightily molested the infidels with arrow and arquebus fire.

The Attack and Defeat of the Infidels

The enemy, selecting five thousand men from among the Spaniards and other nations, formed as many battalions and, raising six different standards, on 13 Ramazan / 7 June marched against the soldiers of Islam. On their part, the courage-emanating *gazis*, putting their trust in God's protection and with cries of *tekbir* and *tahlil* [32] drew their swords and unfurled their banners. The two armies attacked one another, and fought for two hours with such violence that angels in the heavens approved and applauded. With God's help, the believers were victorious. The infidels, defeated, had no choice but to flee, with the warriors in hot pursuit, killing countless numbers of them, while a certain number were taken alive. At that point the troops of Islam reached the enemy's awnings and parapets, raising there their own banners and celebrating. The above-mentioned well was also seized, further weakening the enemy.

A Second Attack of the Infidels

After this battle, as [Muslims] installed fifteen guns in order to start an unceasing bombardment, 3,000 German and Italian armor-clad infidels made an early morning sally from the fortress with the purpose of spiking these guns and overrunning the parapets. The *gazis* were not caught off guard: each stood his ground, offering manly resistance. The infidels reached the guns, and for two hours there was a battle the like of which had never been seen before. In the end here too the attackers, defeated, turned back and fled. The *gazis*, slaying on this occasion seven to eight hundred infidels, stuck their heads on poles and raised them before their [the enemy's] eyes. The infidels who had fled inside resumed the struggle [from there].

Attack of the Gazis *of Islam on the Ships of the Infidels*

The eleven galleys, which had earlier fled and entered the stretch at the base of the fortress, bombarded the [Muslims'] parapets, inflicting much damage. It would have been important from the first to seize them, but besides the fact that [the galleys] lay at anchor beneath the fortress, the shoals extending from that anchorage prevented the ships of the imperial fleet from approaching within the range of their guns—it was not possible to do so [even] with galiots. [So, the following attempt was made:] valiant soldiers and captains armed with bows and arrows, spears, and arquebuses boarded the fleet's *sandals* and *firkatas*, while from landward troops, mounted and well-armed with arquebuses, were assigned to assist them—an assault on [enemy] ships was thus made from several sides. [The defenders] fired from the fortress countless cannonballs, while bullets from arquebuses poured like raindrops, and the *gazis* disappeared in the smoke of all that shooting. To sum it up, fighting went on from dawn till late morning, and many men fell on both sides. The wily infidels erected sturdy stakes in the sea at a distance of a bowshot from the galleys, and by tying the masts and yards with chains they turned the anchorage into a [protected] courtyard-like space. The [above-mentioned boats,] unable to enter it, turned back. In the end, seven or eight guns were installed [by Muslims] on parapets hard by the sea on two sides of the fortress, and as the bombardment [of the ships] from these two sides thickened, most of the infidels were killed, and the rest fell into the water. The [enemy's] guns also became useless wrecks, while their galleys sank up to their wings. The God's oneness confessing *gazis* (*guzat-i muvehhidin*), no longer exposed to fire from enemy guns, resumed the siege of the fortress.

Siege and Conquest of the Fortress and the Extermination of the Infidels

After this battle, at the beginning of Şevval / end of June, [Muslims] proceeded to build [more] parapets; in the process of the siege, their location kept advancing ever closer to the fortress, being changed twenty times. At one point [the existence of] a well with good water was found out about near the trench, from which the infidels, having dug a tunnel to it, were replenishing their supply. Fierce fighting took place over its possession, with many heads cut and blood spilled, until the well was taken from their hands. That was the end of [the infidels'] holding on to any ground outside [the fortress], so that they began to shoot from guns and arquebuses placed on the bastions (*tabyalar*). The soldiers of Islam, making an extreme effort, filled the trench by the bastions, and five high tower-like platforms, built from date-palms and other trees, were erected on as many locations; they surpassed in height the fortress, and guns and arquebuses were lifted upon them. [Muslims] then poured cannonballs and bullets, arrows and stones from them into the interior [of the fortress], not giving [the enemy] a moment of respite. The enemy's battlements and barriers were demolished, the flying debris sending several hundred infidels to hell. Their guns ceased working, and every day five to ten individuals began to flee through the breaches and come [to surrender]. In sum, fighting went on for eighty days in this manner, until at the beginning of Zilkade (end of July) the abject infidels despaired of being rescued. The renowned commander Donabur [Don Álvaro de Sande], whom Spain had sent to conquer kingdoms, who, setting out with the goal of conquering North Africa all the way to Egypt, had entered this fortress with 8800 infidels, now selected one thousand trusted champions and on 7 Zilkade / 30 July, at dawn, made a sally from the fortress, attacking the [Muslims'] parapets. There were three violent clashes, the opponents taking turns in pushing the other one back. Fighting lasted two full hours, with a great number of casualties on both sides. In the end, the infidels could not withstand the attack of the *gazis* nd fled to the fortress. The soldiers of Islam seized its gate and put most of them there to the sword. Their commander, the above-mentioned Donabur, tried to save himself by boarding a galley, but the *gazis* of Islam were on the alert with their *firkatas* and *sandals,* and with God's help the infidel was captured alive. The [enemy's] galleys, after being stripped for booty and too damaged by cannon fire for any use, were burned.

As the infidels in the fortress saw this situation, they raised cries to the heavens asking for mercy, but the *gazis* never considered giving them quarter; with *tekbir* and *tahlil* exclamations, they poured inside through one breach and killed most of them, capturing only a small number; these were put in chains. Once the conquest of the fortress had been completed, [the expedition] stayed three to four days, busy with various matters. After that, on 15 Zilkade / 7 August, [the victors] departed for Tripoli with the purpose of correcting those Arabs in that area who were known for their disloyalty [lit. cowardice; *namerd ile maruf olan Arabların islahi içi*]. Having done that, on the 20th / 12 August [the fleet] set sail for the coast of Rumelia. On 3 Zilhicce / 24 August it arrived at the fortified port of Prevesa, and set out from there, its spirits high [on the return voyage to Istanbul]. On 6 Muharrem 968 / 27 September 1560 it entered the imperial arsenal. The next day the captains and commanders and valiant soldiers who had been captured from the fleet and the fortress of Djerba, 4000 infidels, were presented with their drums, banners, and weapons to the imperial divan. Piyale Pasha and other commanders, donning robes of honor [*kaftan*], were beneficiaries of the sovereign's favor and kindness.

The *Ferah*

Comments on the *Ferah*

Until relatively recently, Kâtip Çelebi's *Tuhfet* was the only major narrative Turkish source used and cited by Turkish and Western scholars alike with respect to the Battle of Djerba. People knew of another, more detailed account, the *Ferah*, written by one Zekeriyyazade, a secretary at the Admiralty, who accompanied Piyale Pasha and served the function of the expedition's bursar. Zekeriyyazade states that he finished writing the account on 3 Safer 968 / 24 October 1560, thus within a month of the fleet's return. No one had made any effort to use the *Ferah* until in 1941 the Italian scholar Alessio Bombaci published a printed edition of the only known manuscript, within the framework of a more comprehensive study, "Le fonti turche della battaglia delle Gerbe (1560)," (*Rivista degli Studi Orientali* 19, nos. 2–4 [1941], pp.193–248, and 20, no. 2 [1942], pp. 279-304). Availing himself of Zekeriyyazade's narrative account as well as of archival documents enabled Bombaci to present an excellent summary of the campaign.

Like the *Tuhfet*, the *Ferah* too has been made more accessible to the Turkish reading public by Orhan Şaik Gökyay's modernized version published in 1975. Perusal of the *Ferah* leaves no doubt that it was Kâtip Çelebi's main source, although perhaps through an unknown intermediary, as Bombaci believes. One thing is certain: the account in the *Tuhfet* is a summary of the much more detailed *Ferah*.

What follows is partly a translation, partly a summary of a few selected segments of the *Ferah*. We have based it both on the Ottoman Turkish original published by Bombaci and on Gökyay's modernized version. Our emphasis is on the early part, which narrates the naval phase of the campaign, from the fleet's departure on 4 April to the naval battle on 13 May. The rest, also detailed and important, deals with the siege of the Djerba fortress; we are including Zekeriyyazade's account of Don Álvaro de Sande's surrender to Piyale Pasha. The folio references are to the only known copy of the manuscript, at Selim Ağa Library in Üsküdar, ms. 768, following those included by Bombaci in his publication of the text.

Translation and Summary of Segments of the *Ferah*

[16a] On this auspicious day of 8 Recep 967 / 4 April 1560, Piyale Pasha, commander of the Ottoman navy, sailed out with a fleet of 74 ships on a campaign. . . . The fleet stayed two days in front of Beşiktaş, by the tomb of that foremost of *gazis*, of warriors who believe in the oneness of God, I mean of His Excellency the *Gazi* Hayreddin Pasha.

[16b] I, the son of a *sipahi*, called Zekeriyyazade, thanks to the honor of being among those who served at the office of His Excellency Rüstem Pasha, rose to the post of scribe at the Imperial Arsenal. While occupying this post, again due to the great kindness of that noble individual, I was ordered to join the expedition in order to disburse the salaries allotted by the sovereign to the crews of the imperial fleet. When the Beylerbeyi of the Fleet Piyale Pasha—may God accord him the fulfillment of his wishes—set out on this auspicious campaign, I sailed with him. Piyale Pasha, Commander of the Navy, is a lion tall as a mountain, a crocodile of the sea. . . . And I stayed by his side at all times, day and night. [17a] . . .

I thus found myself given the chance of entering a special world, when I came to Gallipoli, the gate of combat-seeking warriors and a way station of crocodile-like champions. From there we proceeded to the auspicious fortress of Kilid-i Bahr-i Sefid, one of the two fortresses that guard the Strait [of the Dardanelles]; this one is situated on the European side, and both are marvels on the face of the earth: they protect the lands of the sovereign of Muslim territories and are a thorn in the flank of the polytheists."

Zekeriyyazade then relates the progress of the fleet all the way to Modon at the south-western corner of the Peloponnese. The author mentions no dates between 4 April, when the fleet left Istanbul, and 1 May, when it set out from Modon, but he meticulously records its progress with respect to specific places and activities, some planned, some accidental, but all put to good use under the masterly leadership of Piyale Pasha seconded by his able captains and sailors. We have seen that the imperial fleet had left Istanbul 74 units strong. While proceeding to Modon, and then at Modon itself, this number grew to 120 units through the rallying of *beylik gemileri*, ships under the command of the *beys* of maritime *sancaks*—districts whose function included this type of service.

[23a] . . . His excellency [Piyale] Pasha sent Kurtzade to the nearby harbor of Navarino, with instructions to wait there. The pasha then supervised the gathering of the Pleiad-like numerous soldiers, beys, and *sipahis*, who were distributed among the ships. The armada sailed on Thursday the 5th of the Blessed month of Şaban [1 May 1560] with the intention of confronting the enemy. . . . As the ships left the coast and engaged the open sea, after one or two days land was no longer visible, and the travails of sea voyage made themselves painfully felt for the next two days. With God's help, one night a shore was descried. . . . [24a] Consulting charts, experienced captains knew that it was Malta. They lowered the sails, closed the fleet's formation, and, bewaring of landing at night, waited until morning. At dawn, it was decided to anchor on the lee side of Little Malta. At that point the *gazis* and soldiers went ashore and launched a massive raid of plunder on the island. The infidels wailed and lamented, saying "The devilish Turks!" During this victorious raid individuals were seized for intelligence interrogation. From them it was found out that 'the infidels have not laid siege to Tripoli; instead, they are at Djerba; 49 galleys and 38 *barças* and *karavelas* lie in the shoals off the island. This year they are not worried, saying: "There is no threat from a Turkish fleet, because His Majesty the Fortunate Sovereign, who is

the refuge of the world and whom the mischief-makers— may God strike them down everywhere until Doomsday—call 'Grand Turk,' is embroiled in a quarrel with his young princes, and is preoccupied with putting an end to this disciplinary problem," and that "The Turks are totally ignorant [of our presence]." His excellency the pasha held a council with the beys, and it was decided to send the *firkata* that had come from Turgut Pasha back to him asking him to come to Djerba, the site of the [coming] battle. . . . [Two days later,] through rainstorms and squalls, with great difficulty we came to a shore known as Kerkenna Shoals. We lay there until dawn, when fresh intelligence was received that the fleet of the infidels was nearby, quite unaware [of our approach]. We set out in late morning of the same day. The commanders were ordered to divide into a right and left group in a battle formation. As the fleet advanced, every kind of weapon was made ready and the soldiers prepared for a victorious confrontation. Each person, from high to low, knew that the occasion [also] coincided with the [holy time of] *Kadir Gecesi*.[33] The low and the high all knew for sure that a battle was imminent. Testaments and final instructions were being written without fault. The invocations chanted by the devout so excited the soldiers of Islam that the noisy sea fell silent and started listening. . . . We proceeded in this manner until the time of the evening prayer. The fleet dropped anchor at a place which according to the chart was 12 miles from Djerba. [26a] His excellency the grave, dignified pasha felt the need to proceed in a manner that would be consonant with his sovereign's dignity. He secretly sent out a *firkata* in order to assess the situation of the infidel fleet. It came back with the report that the ships of the accursed infidels were indeed there. At this point the soldiers who believe in God and the warriors who confess His oneness were alerted. The pasha presented them with a variety of favors and promises and all kinds of instructions and advice for the soldiers. By coincidence, it was the *Berat Gecesi*.[34] . . . The crews spent the night until the wee hours of the morning in prayers and thanks to God and His Prophet, recitations of *tesbih, tehlil,* and *zikir.* . . . Meanwhile a frigate came from Malta to the fleet of the accursed infidels with the report that "The Turks' ships have come, leave the fortress, otherwise they will cut your worthless heads, or they will take you into abject captivity." Having heard this, the godless lot immediately made ready to leave in their *barças* and caravels. That meant a fair distance from the shore, out in the sea where they could benefit from the wind. They also took to their galleys, riding at anchor some seven to eight miles out in the sea. As morning approached, they made men climb high up to the mast tops and watch the horizon, so that, should they spot the ships of the imperial fleet, they could be ready. At the break of dawn, there appeared the masts of the imperial fleet thick as a forest. The polytheists—may God keep them low till doomsday—were bewildered; knees shaking, they realized that they could not carry out their nefarious projects. With a thousand efforts, half-dead and with the last remnants of strength, they unfurled their sails and fled. The soldiers of the imperial fleet, seeing that this army of devils was screaming and fleeing, to a man turned into fierce lions. It happened just as the morning prayer was about to end, the ships of Islam put up their sails, the faithful, finishing the prayers, intoned the unison invocations of Muhammad's religion, and the drums of good news were beaten. In their haste, some of our ships didn't even have time to weigh anchor and had to cut the cables. With sails open like angels' wings, they began to catch up. The accursed ones, seeing that, divided their ships into two groups. One struck out into the open sea, the other decided that in order to save their filthy lives it would be better to return to the fortress. [27b] For their part, the ships of the imperial fleet too were divided into two groups. His excellency the Pasha, who slays lions and hunts dragons, set out in pursuit of those that were fleeing seaward; Kara Mustafa Bey and Ali Pertek Bey took on those who were returning to the fortress. One by one, they chased down the ships of the disgraced infidels, while some of the latter, trying to flee, got grounded in the shoals. It was my [lit. this poor one's] luck to reach a swift ship named Alekdo, one of Anton Dorya's ships, my thanks to God's generous gift. The Asaf-like Pasha, upon hearing that I had managed to capture this ship, was very pleased.

Zekeriyyazade thus describes what turned out to be a complete rout of the Christian fleet, some ships sunk, some burnt, some captured, and the crews slain, drowned, or taken prisoner. The author states that 47 ships fell into the hands of the Muslims, two "three-lantern" vessels among them, by which he meant that they belonged to the commanders of the expedition: "One used to belong to the accursed Andrea Doria, and now was the vessel of his son, the naval commander [of the expedition]. He and the Cicilye Kapudanı each boarded a *fırkata* and saved their dirty lives by escaping to the fortress." Among other choice prizes and captures were the "Anabolu Kapudanı with two sons, as well as five of his *barças*, each a one-lantern ship, with troop commanders and captains." Several other ships remained wrecked in the shoals and were left there as a memento to the infidels. The Muslims celebrated their victory by giving thanks to God, ending with the *ükür secdesi* (prostration thanks).

Thus far the naval part of Zekeriyyazade's Cerbe Vakası, or the Battle of Djerba. There followed the almost three months' long siege, until the end of July. At that point Don Álvaro's sally of his select one thousand failed, and the men split up into two groups, one retreating back to the fortress, the other, with Don Álvaro among them, trying to reach the galleys still present in the anchorage. Meanwhile those in the fortress quickly realized the hopelessness of their situation and decided to surrender:

[54a] Even Donabur did not go back to the fortress but slipped away, disappearing among the ships. Many more infidels perished in this attempt. In the end [the infidels in the fortress], unable to withstand the onslaught of the soldiers of Islam, saw their only hope in a *vere* surrender,[35] so they came out and stood there, swords suspended from their mouths, putting shrouds on their necks, helpless, like the dying flame of a candle. Vowing to take oaths after the Muslim fashion, exclaiming "*aman, aman!*" they ranged themselves on the bastions (*tabyalar*).

On our side, as the soldiers of Islam were preparing to launch the

assault, they saw that five strong (*yarar*) infidels, flags of *vere* surrender
in their hands, had come out [54b] of the fortress and headed this
way. His excellency the fortunate Pasha upbraided them, and with the
words "It is too late for a *vere* surrender. We had advised you to do so,
but you did not accept it, oblivious of the consequences," [tried to]
send them back, saying: "Go to your fortress and prepare yourselves
for your time [of reckoning]. Our assault will likely come today or to-
morrow. Why did you come? Here I and my soldiers are ready, go at
once to your posts!" The infidels stood there, distraught and hesitant,
trembling like willow trees, their arms and legs frozen, their tongues
speechless. Bewildered, drained, lifeless, as if spellbound, they remained like that for some time. Then they pulled themselves together
and, weeping and wailing and seeking commiseration (*şefaat*, lit. intercession), they fell to the noble feet of his excellency the pasha: "Kill
whomever you want, we won't go back any more; and we don't insist
on a *vere* surrender either. Becoming your prisoner will be good luck
to us, just as long as our lives are spared, we don't want to die!" The
generous pasha said: "Since you want to be saved in this way, go and
tell all [55a] the infidels, *beys* and captains included, to move to the
inner fortress (*içhisar*), after which you come back; we shall then de-
cide about your fate." One or two of them went there and, carrying
out the order, came back with this information: "In compliance with
your order, they have moved." Meanwhile a [messenger] came with a
report about the ships: "My lord, the ships have been seized and
Donabur captured; they found him there. He is coming here, prisoner and dejected!" What had happened was that Muslim soldiers
and brigades of the religion's army, seeing the people of the fortress
in this situation, raised a thousand expressions of praise and thanks
to God, and rushed to where the ships were, plundering the infidels.
Donabur, who was there at the moment of the plunder (*yağma*), threw
himself into the water, apparently either to drown or, if taken prisoner, to pass unrecognized. However, some warriors from among
those who themselves had been prisoners recognized that accursed
one, saying, "This is the one who was the leader of the trouble-makers

and the source of stubbornness and mischief!" and while the soldiers
of Islam rushed on him, too, ready to make minced meat of him,
[55b] his excellency's captain, Durmuş, happened to be present.
With the help of several [other] captains who had reached the scene
and flocked around him, through a thousand efforts, he saved
[Donabur] from becoming the swords' morsel. Wet from head to toe
like a Jewish duck that had rolled in a rainstorm of calamities,
[Donabur] was brought to the presence of his excellency the great
pasha at that same place where *vere* surrender had been discussed. . .
. The prisoner stood there for a short while, similar to a lifeless image,
voiceless and mute, his appearance miserable, his mind confused.
The incomparable pasha, through an interpreter, told him to sit
down, so he, more bewildered, sat down. Looking at the *beys* who were
sitting by the two sides of his excellency the pasha and at the [other]
grandees standing there, he shook his head. Having composed himself a little, he took off his head cover and ruffled his hair. Exhausted
and slowly turning his face to the ground, he tried to stand up again,
but his excellency the pasha said: "What did you come to do? Stay
longer, *kafir*!" Having understood those words through the interpreter, he replied: "I had no choice, since [56a] the guns placed on
top of one tower killed two to three hundred infidels in one day, perhaps more. From among the things that did us the greatest harm
were those towers." This reply greatly pleased the pasha, for the towers were his idea. He smiled and rendered many thanks and praises
to God for having granted him this splendid victory. As for the other
infidels who were taken prisoner, some degree of discrimination was
observed with respect to their commanders in the matter of food,
drink, and clothing, all of which were provided liberally. Only putting
chains on them was mandatory.

NOTES

1. There is of course the case of another astounding traveler and author, Kâtip Çelebi's contemporary and compatriot Evliya Çelebi. Unlike Ibn Battuta, from a practical standpoint, and Kâtip Çelebi, from an intellectual one, he did not venture beyond the confines of his world, the Ottoman Empire.

2. Thus on p. 21 of the footnoted introduction, there is the following reference: "For information regarding the date of his death see Kâtib Çelebi, *Tuhfetü'l-kibâr*, TSMK, R. 1195, sheet 1a in addition to other sources. For different information on the date of the death of Kâtib Çelebi, see the doctoral dissertation of Z. Aycibin titled *Kâtib Çelebi, Fezleke Tahlil ve Metin I* (Mimar Sinan Güzel Sanatlar Üniversitesi, Sosyal Bilimler Enstitüsü, Istanbul 2007, p. XXIV)." Z. Aycibin's dissertation is listed in the bibliography (p. 187) with the note "basılmamış" (unpublished), but it is probably the most frequently cited reference in the introduction to the English translation. By contrast, the endnotes that accompany the text itself are skimpy and amateurish. The important account of the Djerba campaign, on pp. 100–102, has only one endnote, no. 35: "Giovanni Andrea Doria. Nephew of Andrea Doria. He was the commander of the Genoese fleet in the naval war of Lepanto," while the passage "The Captain of Anabolu and his sons, Andrea Doria's son and the captain of the Sicily Island from among the infidel commanders fled to the frigates with fear for their lives and entered the Jarba Castle" may leave readers somewhat mystified unless helped by a note which at least tells them that Anabolu is Naples (the right procedure would of course have been to use the translated form, Naples, in the text; the translators, however, may have been ignorant of the place's identity). The absence or inadequacy of explanatory notes is occasionally interrupted by painstakingly comprehensive references to manuscript variations, such as the very next one, no. 36: "The additonal text is under the heading 'The Attack of the Muslim Fighters on the Enemy Ships' in Mihrişah Sultan, no. 304, sheets 40b-41a; Lala Ismail, no. 301, sheets 55b-56a; TSMK, R.1189, sheets 131b-132b; TSMK, R.1194, sheet 50b, TSMK, R.1195, sheets 55a-b; Müteferrika edition (sheet 35a) of *Tuhfetü'l-kibâr*, and under the heading 'the Battle of Piyale Pasha with the Fleet of the Infidels' in TSMK, R.1190, sheets 66b-67a and TSMK, R.1193, sheet 42a."

3. The Turkish term is *kapudan, kapudan-ı derya,* or *kapudan paşa,* today usually contracted as *kaptanpaşa.* Moreover, *kapudan* is used for slightly lower ranks as well, while it also can mean governor: thus the viceroy of Sicily becomes *kapudan* in the *Tuhfet.*

4. For a helpful discussion of this very Ottoman term (a loanword from Arabic with the Persian plural suffix – *n*), see Colin Imber, *The Ottoman Empire, 1300–1650: The Structure of Power.* Basingstoke & New York: Palgrave Macmillan, 2002, pp. 303–308 and index, p. 379.

5. *Sandal* is the standard Turkish word for rowboat. Of Byzantine Greek origin, it was created in that language metaphorically from the near-universal word *sandal,* slipper (*Lingua Franca,* #839).

6. The Turkish term *yağlamak* means "to coat a surface with *yağ,* fat, grease, oil." The substance most often used was *don yağı,* "tallow." In English terminology, wooden hulls are painted, not tallowed. However, Colin Heywood tells me that he has found the term *to tallow* used with this connotation in seventeenth-century texts.

7. *Kazak* in Turkish, Ottoman as well as modern, can mean either the Slavic Cossacks or the Turkic Kazakhs. When writing in Turkish, a transliterator of an Ottoman text is thus spared the challenge of deciding which "Kazaks" are meant. The problem surges with a vengeance when a translation has to be made. Those who produced the Ankara translation transformed the Cossacks into Kazakhs.

8. *Shayka* was a boat of moderate size, comparable to the Turkish *kayık,* but lighter and more flat-bottomed, used on the lower courses and estuaries of the great rivers flowing into the Black Sea, from the Danube to the Don. According to *Redhouse Yeni Türkçe-Ingilizce Sözlük,* its etymology is Hungarian.

9. Victor Ostapchuk has recently published several excellent studies on this subject: "Five Documents from the Topkapı Palace Archives on the Ottoman Defence of the Black Sea against the Cossacks," *Journal of Turkish Studies* 2 (1987), pp. 49–104; "The Human Landscape of the Ottoman Black Sea in the Face of the Cossack Naval Raids," *Oriente Moderno* 20:1 (2001), pp. 233–49; "An Ottoman *Gazaname* on Halil Pasha's Naval Campaign against the Cossacks (1621)," *Harvard Ukrainian Studies* 14 (1990), pp. 482–521; and, in Ukrainian, "Kozac'ki chornomorski poxody u morskij istorii Kjatiba Chelebi," *Mappa mundi. Studia in honorem Jaroslavi Dashkevych septuagenario dedicata.* New York, Kiev, Lviv: M. P. Kots, 1996, 341–426.

10. *Korsanlık: Korsan* is a Turkish word of the same origin as the English *corsair* (*Lingua Franca,* #251). In English its meaning can be identical to that of "pirate," but usually there is an important nuance of difference: a corsair

plies his trade not only for profit but also for a higher cause, mostly political or religious, whereas a pirate is a simple sea robber, an outlaw. Corsairs thus become *privateers* in English and *gazis* in Ottoman Turkish. The two (or, in fact, three) causes can overlap or merge: as a corsair, Sir Francis Drake acted on behalf of Queen Elizabeth against Philip II, of his Protestant faith against Catholicism, and for his own enrichment, since capturing Spanish and Portuguese ships laden with American or Oriental treasures was a lucrative business. The same thing can be said, *mutatis mutandis*, of Hayreddin Barbarossa, the most famous seafaring *gazi* of Ottoman history. Modern Turkish has a problem in that it does not differentiate between *corsair* and *pirate*, lumping both in the same word, *korsan*. Only the context reveals which of the two words should be used in a translation, and for the Ottoman *korsanlar* discussed by Kâtip Çelebi it should of course be *corsairs*.

11. This statement is admittedly puzzling. One explanation could be that the text is corrupt.

12. *Reaya*: The Ottoman Empire's ordinary citizens, especially the agriculturists, below the three-level ruling class.

13. *Borda*: The second largest lateen sail on galleys (*Lingua Franca* #109).

14. *Miri kafir*: Infidels who were the *zimmi* citizens of the Ottoman Empire, members of the protected Christian or other minorities, in this case on state or government payroll as oarsmen on galleys.

15. Presumably, the same amount of gunpowder generates greater thrust in the case of guns whose bore is smaller, unless the author means a better-quality gunpowder used by the infidels.

16. *Levent*: Satisfactory translation is difficult because of the special nature of the person it refers to—an inhabitant of Turkey's coastal and insular possessions who serves as a combatant on corsair or naval ships. *Marine* might be the closest rendering in English.

17. This event has received considerable attention in Western historiography. The best examples are the following: Cesáreo Fernández Duro, *Armada Española desde la unión de los reinos de Castilla y de Aragón*, Madrid, 1896, vol. 2, chapter 2: "Los Gelves, 1559–1560," pp. 17–39; Charles Monchicourt, *L'expédition espagnole de 1560 contre l'île de Djerba*, Paris, 1913; R. C. Anderson, *Naval Wars in the Levant, 1559–1853*, Liverpool, 1952, pp. 8–14; Camillo Manfroni, *Storia della Marina Italiana*, vol. 3: Dalla caduta di Costantinopoli alla battaglia di Lepanto, Milano, 1970, pp. 407–22; John Francis Guilmartin, *Gunpowder and Galleys*, London-New York, 1974, pp. 134–43; and Fernand Braudel, "The Djerba Expedition," *The Mediterranean and the Mediterranean World in the Age of Philip II*, vol. 2, trans. Siân Reynolds. New York: Harper &

Row, 1973, pp. 973–87.

18. Piyale Pasha is no. 15 on Kâtip Çelebi's list of grand admirals in chapter 1 of the second part: "Piyale Pasha. Of Croatian stock. He left the Imperial Harem in 954 / 1547 to assume the position of Head Gate Keeper (*Kapıcı Ba ı*), and in 962 / 1554 he became grand admiral with the *sancak* of Gallipoli [as his fief]. In 967 / 1560, given the rank (*paye*) of *beylerbeyi* of Cezayir, he conquered Djerba and, bringing [as prisoner] the captain of Naples, became an inlaw (*damad*) of prince (*ehzade*) Selim. In 973 / 1566 he conquered Sakiz (Chios), and was rewarded with the rank of vizier. In 975 / 1567, with a *has* level income, he rose to the rank of third vizier. He died on 13 Zilkade 985 / 29 April 1578. He is buried in the courtyard of his mosque in Kasımpa a. The chronogram of his death is '*Çekmis ecel dolusun nagâh Piyale Pa a*' ('Piyale Pasha suddenly quaffed the fill of his allotted time'). He occupied the post of admiral (*kapudan*) for fourteen years. He built a mosque and a bath. His garden in Üsküdar was one of the wonders of the world." An expanded and slightly different paragraph on this remarkable personality is offered by Ismail Hami Dani mend in his book *Osmanlı Devlet Erkân* (Istanbul: Türkiye Yayınevi, 1971), pp. 181–82. Listed as no. 29, Piyale Pasha is described as probably being of Hungarian origin, on the premise that he had been acquired as a child during Süleyman the Magnificent's campaign that was crowned with the victory at Mohács in 1526. His promotion to the rank of third vizier made him a *kubbe veziri*, the inner group of ministers constituting the council of state formally meeting in a domed (*kubbe*) pavilion at Topkapı Palace, with the sultan usually in discreet attendance. Although this promotion put an end to his function as grand admiral, he actively participated in the conquest of Cyprus, overshadowing the mediocre *kaptanpasa* Müezzinzade Ali.

19. Andrea Doria (1466–1560) was a Genoese patrician and naval commander who in 1528 entered Habsburg service. He lived long enough to learn of the disaster that befell the fleet under the command of his grand-nephew Gian-Andrea Doria, for he died on 25 November.

20. According to Duro, *Armada Española*, p. 20, the Turkish garrison had meanwhile been bolstered with two thousand men sent together with more armaments and provisions from Istanbul, and Tripoli's defenses were being reinforced. Even so, the ten thousand troops on board the Christian expeditionary force might have been sufficient, especially if joined by local Arab leaders.

21. Monchicourt, *L'Expédition Espagnole*, p. 109, quoting Anton Francesco Cirni, *Successi dell'armata della Mta Cca Destinata all'Impresa di Tripoli di Barbe-*

ria, Della presa delle Gerbe e progressi dell'armata Turchesca, Florence, 1560: "*Un bel fuggire vale più che un bravo combattere.*" Like Zekeriyyazade's, Cirni's is an eyewitness account.

22. "Capitán general de la empresa" is the title we find in Spanish sources.

23. Zekeriyyazade, however, not only mentions the flight of the "kapudan of Sicily" but relates in great detail the abuse heaped on Medinaceli by his wife for leaving a son of his behind. This was Don Gastón de la Cerda, the duke's second son, who then died in Istanbul. Duro, *Armada Española,* vol. 2, p. 35.

24. Duro, *Armada Española,* vol. 2, p. 38.

25. In reality there were only 74 galleys at the moment of departure from Be ikta . The number grew to 120 through the above-mentioned system of the governors of maritime *sancaks* joining the imperial fleet on a campaign.

26. Koyun Adaları ("Sheep Islands") is the name of a small archipelago between Chios and the Turkish coast; the islands are known in Greek as Oinoussa and in Italian as Spalmadori.

27. The future grand admiral, in which position he was renamed as Kılıç Ali.

28. *Barça* had the fairly generic connotation of a large sailing ship used for freight and troop transport purposes, in contrast to the *kalyon*, its more strictly military counterpart, but both the terms and the types overlapped to a degree.

29. Gozzo, a smaller island some five kilometers to the northwest of Malta.

30. The text says "200 miles east of Tripoli." The error may well be the author's, because it is found in all the manuscripts we have seen.

31. *Tabur* should mean a defense line formed with wagons chained to one another that could at the same time serve as platforms for light artillery, a system first developed by Czechs in the Hussite wars of the 1420s. In Turkish, the term must have acquired a broader meaning, for here it is applied to a situation where wagons could hardly have made an appearance.

32. "God is Great!" and "There is no God but Allah!"

33. *Kadir Gecesi:* Night of Power, 26/27 Ramazan, the time of the first revelation of the Qur'an.

34. *Berat Gecesi:* Night of Promise, 14/15 Şaban, a sacred night also known as *Berat Kandili.*

35. *Vere* meant capitulation accepted by the besieger, and it usually included conditions, the principal of which was that the lives of those who had surrendered would be spared.

BIBLIOGRAPHY

Anderson, Roger Charles. *Naval Wars in the Levant, 1559–1853.* Liverpool: At the University Press, 1952.

Bostan, Idris. *Osmanlı Bahriye Te kilâtı: XVII. Yüzyılda Tersâne-i Âmire.* Ankara: Türk Tarih Kurumu Basımevi, 1992.

———. *Kürekli ve Yelkenli Osmanlı Gemileri.* Istanbul: Bilge, 2005.

Braudel, Fernand. *The Mediterranean and the Mediterranean World in the Age of Philip II,* vol. 2. Trans. Siân Reynolds. New York: Harper & Row, 1973, pp. 973–87.

Dani mend, Ismail Hakkı. *Osmanlı Devlet Erkânı.* Istanbul: Türkiye Yayınevi, 1971.

Duro, Cesáreo Fernández. *Armada Española Desde la Unión de los Reinos de Castilla y de Aragón,* vol. 2. Madrid: Est. tipografico "Sucesores de Rivadeneyra," 1896.

Gökyay, Orhan Şaik. *Kâtip Çelebi: Ya amı, Ki iliği ve Eserlerinden Seçmeler.* [Ankara]: Türkiye I Bankası Kültür Yayınları, 1982.

Guilmartin, John Francis. *Gunpowder & Galleys: Changing Technology and Mediterranean Warfare at Sea in the 16th Century.* London: Cambridge University Press, 1974.

Hagen, Gottfried. *Ein Osmanischer Geograph bei der Arbeit: Entstehung und Gedankenwelt von K tib elebis ih nnüm .* Berlin: Klaus Schwarz Verlag, 2003.

Imber, Colin. "The Navy of Süleyman the Magnificent." *Archivum Ottomanicum* 6 (1980), pp. 211–82.

———. *The Ottoman Empire, 1300–1650: The Structure of Power,* 2nd ed., especially chapter 8: "The Fleet." Basingstoke & New York: Palgrave Macmillan, 2009.

Kahane, Henry, Renée Kahane, and Andreas Tietze. *The Lingua Franca in the Levant: Turkish Nautical Terms of Italian and Greek Origin.*

Urbana: University of Illinois Press, 1958.

Manfroni, Camillo. *Storia della Marina Italiana*, vol. 3. Milano: Periodici scientifici, 1970.

Monchicourt, Charles. *L'Expédition Espagnole de 1560 contre l'Île de Djerba*. Paris: E. Leroux, 1913.

Naima, Mustafa. *Tarih-i Naima*, vol. 6. Istanbul: Matbaa-yı Âmire, 1280 [1863].

Ostapchuk, Victor. "Five Documents from the Topkapı Palace Archives on the Ottoman Defence of the Black Sea against the Cossacks." *Journal of Turkish Studies* 2 (1987), pp. 49–104.

————. "An Ottoman *Gazaname* on Halil Pasha's Naval Campaign against the Cossacks (1621)." *Harvard Ukrainian Studies* 14 (1990), pp. 482–521.

————. "Kozac'ki chornomorski poxody u morskij istorii Kjatiba Chelebi." *Mappa mundi: Studia in honorem Jaroslavi Dashkevych septuagenario dedicata*. New York, Kiev, Lviv: M. P. Kots, 1996, pp. 341–426.

————. "The Human Landscape of the Ottoman Black Sea in the Face of the Cossack Naval Raids." *Oriente Moderno* 20:1 (2001), pp. 233–49.

Soucek, Svatopluk. "The Rise of the Barbarossas in North Africa." *Archivum Ottomanicum* 3 (1971), pp. 238–50.

————. "Certain Types of Ships in Ottoman-Turkish Terminology." *Turcica* 7 (1975), pp. 233–49.

————. "Naval Aspects of the Ottoman Conquest of Rhodes, Cyprus and Crete." *Studia Islamica* 98/99 (2004), pp. 219–61.

Uzunçarşılı, Ismail Hakkı. *Osmanlı Devletinin Merkez ve Bahriye Teşkilâtı*, 2nd printing. Ankara: Türk Tarih Kurumu, 1984.

CPSIA information can be obtained at www.ICGtesting.com
Printed in the USA
BVOW041947141111

276085BV00001B/14/P